4 All-Star

Workbook

Linda Lee ★ Stephen Sloan ★
Grace Tanaka ★ Shirley Velasco

Workbook by Linda Lee and Kristin Sherman

McGraw-Hill

All-Star 4 Workbook, 1st Edition

Published by McGraw-Hill ESL/ELT, a business unit of The McGraw-Hill Companies, Inc. 1221 Avenue of the Americas, New York, NY 10020. Copyright © 2006 by The McGraw-Hill Companies, Inc. All rights reserved. No part of this publication may be reproduced or distributed in any form or by any means, or stored in a database or retrieval system, without the prior written consent of The McGraw-Hill Companies, Inc., including, but not limited to, in any network or other electronic storage or transmission, or broadcast for distance learning.

ISBN 0-07-284688-7
1 2 3 4 5 6 7 8 9   QPD/QPD   11 10 09 08 07 06 05

ISBN 0-07-111726-1 (International Workbook)
1 2 3 4 5 6 7 8 9   QPD/QPD   11 10 09 08 07 06 05

Editorial director: Tina Carver
Executive editor: Erik Gundersen
Developmental editor: Jennifer Monaghan
Production manager: MaryRose Malley
Interior designer: Wee Design Group
Cover designer: Wee Design Group
Art: Andrew Lange; NETS/Carlos Sanchis

INTERNATIONAL EDITION ISBN 0-07-111726-1
Copyright © 2006. Exclusive rights by The McGraw-Hill Companies, Inc., for manufacture and export. This book cannot be re-exported from the country to which it is sold by McGraw-Hill. The International Edition is not available in North America.

The **McGraw·Hill** Companies

All-Star is a four-level, standards-based series for English learners featuring a picture-dictionary approach to vocabulary building. "Big picture" scenes in each unit provide springboards to a wealth of activities developing all of the language skills. Each *All-Star* Workbook unit provides 20 pages of supplementary exercises for its corresponding Student Book unit. The Workbook activities offer students further practice in developing the language, vocabulary, and life-skill competencies taught in the Student Book. Answers to the Workbook activities are available in the Teacher's Edition.

Features

★ **Wide range of exercises** can be used by students working independently or in groups, in the classroom, with a tutor, or at home. Each lesson includes at least one activity which allows students to interact, usually by asking and answering questions.

★ **Alternate application lessons** complement the Student Book application lesson, inviting students to tackle work, family, and/or community extension activities in each unit. Each application lesson concludes with a *Take It Outside* activity or a *Take It Online* activity, or both. *Take It Outside* activities encourage students to use the language skills they've learned in the unit to interact with others outside of the classroom. *Take It Online* activities offer suggestions for web-based activities. These activities help students build computer skills while expanding on the content and the language skills they learned in the unit.

★ **Student Book page references** at the top of each Workbook page show how the two components support one another.

★ **Practice tests** at the end of each unit provide practice answering multiple-choice questions such as those found on the CASAS tests. Students are invited to chart their progress on these tests on a bar graph on the inside back cover.

★ **Spotlight: Reading** lessons appear at the end of every unit, offering supplementary reading practice which builds on the reading strategies introduced in the Student Book.

★ **Spotlight: Writing** lessons appear at the end of every unit, offering supplementary writing practice which builds on the writing strategies introduced in the Student Book.

Alternate Application Lessons (work, family, community)

Equipped for the Future (EFF) is a set of standards for adult literacy and lifelong learning, developed by The National Institute for Literacy (www.nifl.gov). The organizing principle of EFF is that adults assume responsibilities in three major areas of life—as workers, as parents, and as citizens. These three areas of focus are called "role maps" in the EFF documentation.

Lesson 6 in each unit of the Student Book provides a real-life application relating to one of the learners' roles. The Workbook includes two lessons, each of which addresses the other roles. This allows you, as the teacher, to customize the unit to meet the needs of your students. You can teach any or all of the application lessons in class. For example, if all your students work, you may choose to focus on the work applications. If your students have diverse interests and needs, you may have them work in small groups on different applications. If your program provides many hours of classroom time each week, you have enough material to cover all three roles.

Contents

Unit 5 Consumer News and Views

Unit 6 Rules and Laws

What skills do you want to learn?

A Unscramble the questions. Then use the course schedule to answer the questions.

1. does / meet / the keyboarding class / when

   _When does the keyboarding class meet?_____

   _It meets from 7 to 8._____

2. the computer repair class / when / begin / does

   _____ ?

   _____ .

3. which course / the cheapest / is

   _____ ?

   _____ .

4. the most expensive / are / which two courses

   _____ ?

   _____ .

5. the writing course / weeks / does / how many / last

   _____ ?

   _____ .

6. how much / to take / writing II / would it cost / and keyboarding

   _____ ?

   _____ .

7. do students / in which courses / probably use computers

   _____ ?

   _____ .

8. improve your health / might help you / which courses

   _____ ?

   _____ .

Continuing Education Course Schedule
Wednesday Evening Classes

COURSE	WKS	TIME	TUITION	
Auto Body Repair	12	6:30–9:30	$145	B3
Basic Computer Skills	10	7:00–9:00	$124	B307
Careers in Banking	8	6:30–9:00	$109	B223
Computer Repair	10	6:30–9:30	$149	B234
Defensive Driving	1	7:45–10:00	$45	PE22
Drawing Workshop	8	6:30–9:00	$124	W453
Interviewing Skills	12	6:00–9:00	$165	Th43
Italian Cooking	10	7:00–8:30	$89	B304
Keyboarding	8	7:00–8:00	$120	B231
Photography	8	6:45–9:45	$149	B303
Pottery I	10	6:00–8:30	$109	B308
Public Speaking	8	7:00–9:00	$109	B302
Small Engine Repair	12	7:00–9:00	$165	B306
Stress Management	12	4:00–5:00	$89	W233
Tai Chi	10	7:00–8:30	$75	B305
Writing II	10	7:00–9:00	$124	B301

B In which classes might you hear someone say the things below?

1. Are there any more aprons? _____ *Italian cooking and pottery* _____
2. Which button should I push? _____
3. Did you turn the oven on? _____
4. Could you please turn the light off? _____
5. How does it taste? _____
6. I need to wash my hands. _____

C Choose an adjective to complete each sentence below. (More than 1 answer is possible.)

interesting	important	helpful
boring	unimportant	unhelpful
useful	common	necessary
useless	unusual	unnecessary

1. Knowing how to cook is a very _____ skill.
2. It's _____ to learn how to make pottery.
3. Knowing how to speak in public is _____ for supervisors.
4. Knowing how to use a computer is _____ for teachers.
5. It's _____ for everyone to know how to manage stress.
6. It's _____ to know how to use a keyboard if you want to use a computer.
7. Knowing how to repair engines is very _____.
8. It's _____ to improve your interviewing skills before you go for a job interview.
9. I think it would be _____ to work in a bank.
10. It's _____ for children to study a foreign language.

D Choose a profession and a skill to complete each question below. Then circle your answer.

	Professions			Skills	
teacher	mechanic	photographer	drive a car	speak a foreign language
doctor	waiter	file clerk	add and subtract	give clear instructions
farmer	tailor	reporter	repair equipment	read

1. Do you think a _____ needs to know how to _____? YES NO
2. Does a _____ need to know how to _____? YES NO
3. Do you think a _____ needs to know how to _____? YES NO
4. Does a _____ need to know how to _____? YES NO

3

Skills for Success

LESSON 2

A Add the missing words to the chart and complete the questions below. Then answer the questions.

ADJECTIVES	ADVERBS
1.	essentially
2. clear	
3. concise	
4.	proficiently
5.	responsibly
6.	cooperatively
7. different	
8. good	
9.	possibly
10.	easily

1. What is _____*essential*_____ for all children to have? _____

2. Was the sky _____ yesterday? _____

3. Is it important to give instructions _____ in an emergency? _____

4. How long does it take to become a _____ driver? _____

5. Who is _____ for cooking in your family? _____

6. Why is it sometimes difficult to work _____? _____

7. How is English _____ from your first language? _____

8. What do you wish you could do _____? _____

9. Is it _____ for an immigrant to become a U.S. senator or representative? _____

10. What sport is _____ to learn how to play? _____

B Match the words that are similar in meaning. Write the words on the lines.

1. necessary _____*essential*_____

2. act _____

3. skillful _____

4. focus _____

5. understand _____

6. answer _____

7. brief _____

8. think of _____

9. get better _____

a. concentrate

b. come up with

c. concise

d. improve

e. proficient

f. comprehend

g. respond

h. essential

i. behave

j. cooperate

C Complete the sentences with words from the box.

distracted	behavior	affect	left out
share	resolved	encourage	interact
focused	interpersonal	proficient	come up with

1. Five people live in my apartment; each person pays an equal _____ of the rent.

2. The cake tasted very strange because the chef _____ the eggs.

3. The noise of the children _____ me from my work.

4. What are the rules of _____ in the library?

5. Most people look down at the floor when they are riding in an elevator; they don't _____ with the other people in the elevator.

6. A _____ public speaker can speak clearly and concisely.

7. Jim and Bob weren't able to work together until they _____ their differences.

8. Eating less food should _____ your weight.

9. People with poor _____ skills have trouble getting along with others.

10. It took us several weeks to _____ a name for our restaurant.

11. My parents wanted me to become a doctor. They didn't _____ me to become an actor.

12. In my speech, I _____ on the causes of the war; I didn't talk about the effects.

D What skills are important in each profession below? Check (✓) the 3 most important skills for each one. Then complete the sentences below.

	Interpersonal Skills	Listening Skills	Problem-Solving Skills	Speaking Skills	Team Skills	Writing Skills
Police officer	✓		✓	✓		
Taxi driver						
Salesperson						
Receptionist						
Nurse						
Construction worker						

1. I think a police officer needs to have good _____*problem solving*_____ skills because _____*different things*_____ *happen every day on the job.*

2. I think a taxi driver needs to have good _____ skills because _____

3. In my opinion, a receptionist needs to have good _____ skills because _____

4. I think a _____ should have good _____ skills because _____

5

3 LESSON

Are you listening?

A Number each conversation in order starting with #1.

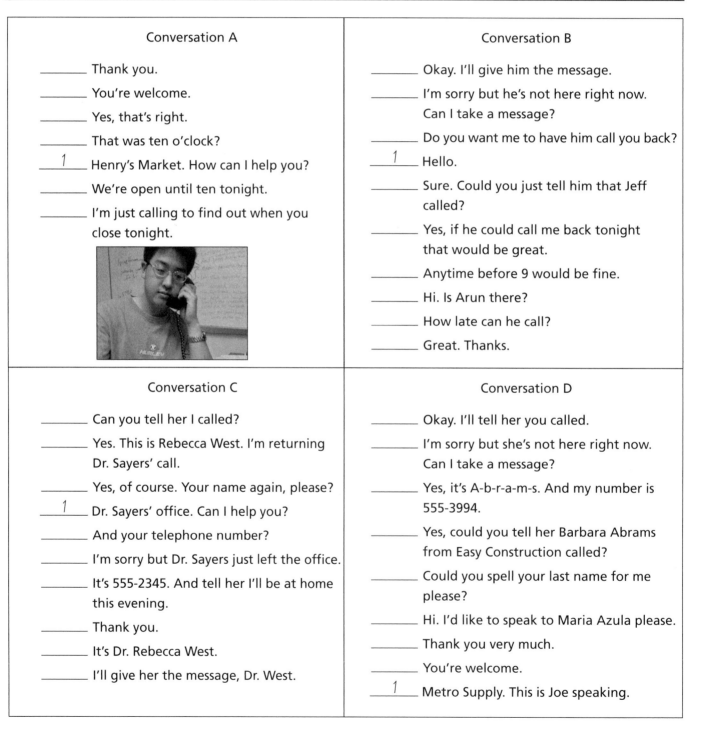

Conversation A

_____ Thank you.

_____ You're welcome.

_____ Yes, that's right.

_____ That was ten o'clock?

___1___ Henry's Market. How can I help you?

_____ We're open until ten tonight.

_____ I'm just calling to find out when you close tonight.

Conversation B

_____ Okay. I'll give him the message.

_____ I'm sorry but he's not here right now. Can I take a message?

_____ Do you want me to have him call you back?

___1___ Hello.

_____ Sure. Could you just tell him that Jeff called?

_____ Yes, if he could call me back tonight that would be great.

_____ Anytime before 9 would be fine.

_____ Hi. Is Arun there?

_____ How late can he call?

_____ Great. Thanks.

Conversation C

_____ Can you tell her I called?

_____ Yes. This is Rebecca West. I'm returning Dr. Sayers' call.

_____ Yes, of course. Your name again, please?

___1___ Dr. Sayers' office. Can I help you?

_____ And your telephone number?

_____ I'm sorry but Dr. Sayers just left the office.

_____ It's 555-2345. And tell her I'll be at home this evening.

_____ Thank you.

_____ It's Dr. Rebecca West.

_____ I'll give her the message, Dr. West.

Conversation D

_____ Okay. I'll tell her you called.

_____ I'm sorry but she's not here right now. Can I take a message?

_____ Yes, it's A-b-r-a-m-s. And my number is 555-3994.

_____ Yes, could you tell her Barbara Abrams from Easy Construction called?

_____ Could you spell your last name for me please?

_____ Hi. I'd like to speak to Maria Azula please.

_____ Thank you very much.

_____ You're welcome.

___1___ Metro Supply. This is Joe speaking.

B Use Conversations C and D on page 6 to complete the telephone messages.

WHILE YOU WERE OUT

FOR: _____
DATE: 1/23   TIME: 10:30 a.m.
FROM: _____
OF: _____
PHONE: _____
EMAIL: _____

☐ Telephoned   ☐ Will Call Again
☐ Returned Call   ☐ Please See Me
☐ Please Call   ☐ Important

MESSAGE: _____
_____
_____

WHILE YOU WERE OUT

FOR: _____
DATE: 2/18   TIME: 10:30 a.m.
FROM: _____
OF: _____
PHONE: _____
EMAIL: _____

☐ Telephoned   ☐ Will Call Again
☐ Returned Call   ☐ Please See Me
☐ Please Call   ☐ Important

MESSAGE: _____
_____
_____

C Complete the sentences with *should* or *shouldn't*.

1. You _____ speak clearly when you talk on the telephone.
2. You _____ use words such as "you guys" on the telephone at work.
3. You _____ talk on your cell phone in a restaurant.
4. You _____ leave long messages on a telephone answering machine.
5. You _____ speak softly on a cell phone when you are on a bus or train.
6. You _____ identify yourself when you leave a message on an answering machine.
7. You _____ put someone on hold for a long time.
8. You _____ always say "Goodbye" before you hang up the phone.

D Complete the answering machine messages with your own ideas.

1.

"Hi _____. This is your employee _____. I'm calling to _____. Please call me back when you have a chance. My number is _____. Thank you. Bye."

2.

"Hi _____. This is _____. I'm calling to _____
_____
_____

Thanks. Bye."

7

How well do you write?

LESSON 4

A Complete the questions with words from the box. Then answer the questions.

accurate	according to	clarity	scan
complex	assess	demand	improve
up to	promote	quote	decide

1. Are you _____ climbing five flights of stairs? _____

2. _____ you, what is the most important skill for all employees to have? _____

3. How do employers decide who to _____ ? _____

4. Why has the _____ for people with good writing skills increased?_____

_____

5. Why do newspaper reporters often _____ other people in their articles?_____

_____

6. Is your watch _____? _____

7. How do employers _____ who to hire? _____

8. Which is more important in writing—accuracy or _____? _____

9. Do you enjoy filling out _____ forms? _____

10. How can you _____ your progress in learning English? _____

11. What can you do to _____ your writing skills?_____

12. What might you _____ rather than read carefully? _____

B There are 3 spelling mistakes in the e-mail message below. Circle the mistakes and then write the words correctly on the lines to the right.

Inbox	Reply	Reply All	Forward	Print	Delete

From: Smith, Jim <SmiJi@vesper.net   To: Hue, Tina <Tina_Hue@suncast.net
Subject: Meating on Friday   CC: Otto, Sam <OtSa@vesper.net

Hi:

Can we change the time of Friday's meeting? Sam and I are both free at 2 p.m. Woud that work for you? If 2 isn't good for you, we'll have to postpone the meeting until nekt week.

Jim

_____

_____

_____

C Add the missing job title to each job description. Write the job titles on the lines.

JOB TITLES
Bilingual Receptionist   Staff Supervisor   Line Cook   Carpenter Helper

Job Title: _____
Job Description:
This cooking position requires good communication and team skills. Hotel cooking experience and a culinary degree preferred. Professional knowledge of cooking, ingredients, and procedures preferred.
Job classification: Full Time
Education: High School Diploma or GED
Job Benefits:
Clothing / Uniform Allowance   Dental Insurance
Health Insurance   Sick Leave

Job Title: _____
Job Description:
Position requires a minimum of three years' supervisory experience in a customer service environment, preferably in the travel industry. The successful candidate will have excellent English written / verbal communication and organizational skills. PC literacy and Bachelor's degree required; fluency in several languages a plus.
Job classification: Full Time
Education: Bachelor's Degree
Job Benefits:
401K / Retirement Plan   Health Insurance
Annual Bonus   Paid Vacation

Job Title: _____
Job Description:
Hospitality organization is seeking a strong bilingual receptionist to work in a front desk position. Candidates should be bilingual in English and Spanish, have strong customer service skills, and good writing skills. In addition, candidates should be able to work independently.
Job classification: Full Time
Education: High School Diploma or GED
Job Benefits:
Health Insurance   Sick Leave   Vacation

Job Title: _____
Job Description:
Local stairway fabricator has openings for qualified framers. Interested applicants should have some type of carpentry background, be able to read job orders / blueprints, be able to work on a team, and have good measuring skills.
Job classification: Full Time
Education: High School Diploma or GED
Job Benefits:
No benefit package available.

D Use the job descriptions in Activity C to answer the questions below.

	Line Cook	Staff Supervisor	Bilingual Receptionist	Carpenter Helper
1. Which job requires a college degree?	☐	☐	☐	☐
2. Which job is full time?	☐	☐	☐	☐
3. Which job requires good team skills?	☐	☐	☐	☐
4. Which job provides health insurance?	☐	☐	☐	☐
5. Which job requires good writing skills?	☐	☐	☐	☐
6. Which job requires good communication skills?	☐	☐	☐	☐

5 LESSON

Do you know if she's here?

A Complete the questions below.

1. Do you know if she _____ to class every day? (go)

2. Do you know if the president _____ Spanish? (speak)

3. Can you tell me if this sentence _____ clear? (be)

4. Do you know if she _____ her promotion yesterday? (get)

5. Do you know if anyone here _____ to class yesterday? (go)

6. Do you know if the stores _____ open now? (be)

7. Do you remember if we _____ homework yesterday? (have)

8. Can you tell me if I _____ this form accurately? (fill out)

9. Do you know if she _____ still sick? (be)

10. Do you know if she _____ her driving test yesterday? (pass)

B Rewrite each direct question as an indirect question.

1. Is he a good problem solver?

   Do you know if he is a good problem solver?

2. Is she taking a computer course?

   _____

3. Is she a good doctor?

   _____

4. Is he a proficient writer?

   _____

5. Was he born here?

   _____

6. Was she late to class?

   _____

7. Was the speech clear?

   _____

8. Does she speak more than one language?

   _____

9. Did they do their share of the work?

   _____

10. Did Jane come up with the solution?

_____

C Match each question to an answer. Write the letter of the answer on the line.

1. Do you know when California became a state? _____
2. Can you tell me who the first U.S. President was? _____
3. Do you know who wrote the U.S. national anthem (the Star Spangled Banner)? _____
4. Can you tell me what the Emancipation Proclamation did? _____
5. Do you know when the American Revolution began? _____
6. Do you know who invented the light bulb? _____
7. Do you know what the capital of the U.S. is? _____
8. Do you know how many states there are in the U.S.? _____

   a. Yes. It freed the slaves.
   b. Yes. It was Thomas Edison.
   c. Yes. It was Frances Scott Key.
   d. Yes. It was in 1850.
   e. Yes. It was George Washington.
   f. Yes. It began in 1775.
   g. Yes. There are fifty.
   h. Yes, I do. It's Washington D.C.

D Unscramble the indirect questions. Then answer them.

1. (is / the capital / do you know / of Canada / what)

   Indirect question: _Do you know what the capital of Canada is?_____

   Answer: _____

2. (the minimum voting age / is / what / in the United States / can you tell me)

   Indirect question: _____?

   Answer: _____.

3. do you know / are / the colors / what / of / the U.S. flag

   Indirect question: _____?

   Answer: _____.

4. today / the Vice President / can you tell me / who / is / of the United States

   Indirect question: _____?

   Answer: _____.

5. the governor / of our state / is / now / who / do you know

   Indirect question: _____?

   Answer: _____.

FAMILY

LESSON

What do teachers want parents to do?

A For each category below, add 2 more examples.

Category	Examples
1) Ways parents can be involved in their children's education	• they can volunteer at school • •
2) Ways parents can discipline their children	• they can take something away • •
3) Way parents can encourage their children to read	• they can praise them • •

B Read the article below. How important do you think it is for parents to do each thing? Write *VI (very important), SI (somewhat important),* or *NI (not important)* on the lines.

Eight Things Teachers Wish Parents Would Do
Brought to you by the National PTA®

1. **Be involved.** Parent involvement helps students learn, improves schools, and helps teachers work with you to help your children succeed. _____

2. **Provide resources at home for learning.** Use your local library, and have books and magazines available in your home. Read with your children each day. _____

3. **Set a good example.** Show your children by your own actions that you believe reading is both enjoyable and useful. Monitor[1] television viewing. _____

4. **Encourage students to do their best in school.** Show your children that you believe education is important and that you want them to do their best. _____

5. **Value education and seek a balance[2] between schoolwork and outside activities.** Emphasize[3] your children's progress in developing the knowledge and skills they need to be successful both in school and in life. _____

6. **Support school rules and goals.** Take care not to undermine[4] school rules, discipline, or goals. _____

7. **Use pressure[5] positively.** Encourage children to do their best, but don't pressure them by setting goals too high or by scheduling too many activities. _____

8. **Call teachers early if you think there's a problem.** Call while there is still time to solve the problem. Don't wait for teachers to call you. _____

---

[1]monitor: observe, watch over

[2]balance: not too much of one or the other

[3]emphasize: place importance on

[4]undermine: ruin the efforts of

[5]pressure: the making of demands

Excerpted from "Top Ten Things Teachers Wish Parents Would Do" from www.familyeducation.com. Used with permission from National PTA, www.pta.org.

C Which of the suggestions from Activity B are these parents following? Write your answers.

1. Sonya reads to her children before they go to bed every night.
   She provides resources at home for learning.

2. When Tomi's children were young, she almost never watched TV.

   _____

3. Regina and Paolo praise their daughter a lot when she gets good grades.

   _____

4 Marie volunteers at her children's school three hours a week. She usually helps out in the library.

   _____

5. Ali's son suddenly stopped doing his homework at school. Ali called his son's teachers right away to find out if something had happened at school.

   _____

D Choose the correct form of the words to complete the questions. Then ask a classmate.

NOUN	VERB	ADJECTIVE
1. involvement	involve	XXXXX
2. success	succeed	successful
3. action	act	active
4. enjoyment	enjoy	enjoyable
5. encouragement	encourage	XXXXX
6. education	educate	educational
7. support	support	supportive
8. discipline	discipline	disciplinary

1. What _____ should grandparents have in their grandchildren's education?
2. What is the secret to being a _____ parent?
3. Why are some children more _____ than others?
4 Do you think going to the library is _____?
5. How can you _____ children to do their homework?
6. How important is it to get a good _____?
7. Who gave you a lot of _____ when you were a child?
8. In the U.S., what are unacceptable ways to _____ a child?

TAKE IT ONLINE: Use your favorite search engine to look for information about parenting skills. Write down 3 interesting things you learn.

1. _____

2. _____

3. _____

Get Involved in Your Community

A Read questions 1 and 2. Look for the answers in the article below. Write your answers on the lines.

1. What are 2 things the article tells you about Maria Gomez?

   _____

   _____

2. What are 4 things the article tells you about the Community Volunteers in the Schools Program?

   _____   _____

   _____   _____

San Francisco School Volunteers

When Maria Gomez was in the second grade, someone told her she could be a doctor. Today, Dr. Gomez heads a health clinic and goes back to the second grade as a volunteer for three hours a week.

You don't have to be a doctor to be inspirational and you don't have to be a rocket scientist to know that your time at a public school can mean the difference between success and failure for a child.

The Community Volunteers in the Schools Program helps people like Dr. Gomez get connected with children in a school. This program orients volunteers to the schools, places them with a school that is convenient for them, and follows up to make sure volunteer placements are successful. Annually, 2000 volunteers are placed through this program.

These volunteers do everything from listening to a child read to using beads or cubes to reinforce math concepts to assisting in the computer lab. Their help does make a difference. In year-end surveys, almost 98% of teachers who have a volunteer say they want one again next year.

Requests for volunteers continue to grow. There is an urgent need for volunteers for the fall, particularly volunteers who have a second language ability in Spanish or Chinese. All it takes is two to three hours a week during the school year. What you get is the satisfaction of knowing you made a difference. We think that's not a bad return on a small investment.

From "Community Volunteers in the School," www.sfsv.org. Reprinted by permission of the San Francisco School Volunteers.

B Answer the questions using information from Activity A.

1. What does Maria Gomez do for work?

_____

2. What is the purpose of the Community Volunteers in Schools Program?

_____

3. What do some volunteers in the program do?

_____

C Read the Community Bulletin Board. What skills and abilities would you need to volunteer for each job? Add your ideas to the chart below.

COMMUNITY BULLETIN BOARD
Volunteers Needed

Cleaners and Painters
Volunteers are needed for interior and exterior cleaning and painting of the Oliver House. Work planned for July 5 & 6 at 7 A.M. to noon.
Contact: Josh Hagar at 555-5694

Meal Delivery
Any number of hours you can help out each week will be greatly appreciated. Volunteers are needed to deliver meals to homebound seniors. Car and driver's license necessary.
Contact: Rhonda Smith, Taylor Senior Center, 555-9485

Santa Claus
Someone to dress as Santa and give out treats at the Annual Festival of Lights at the Randolf Center on Dec. 1st from 6 P.M. to 7 P.M.
Contact: Shirley, Non-Profit Organization, 555-9948

Manicurist
Give manicures to residents in a long-term care facility. Thursday 3 P.M.
Contact: Deborah Simons 555-4939

Cleaners/Painters	Meal Delivery	Santa Claus	Manicurist
climb a ladder *follow instructions*			

★★★

TAKE IT OUTSIDE: Look in a local newspaper for volunteer opportunities in your area. Bring any information you find to class and share it with your classmates.

★★★

TAKE IT ONLINE: Use your favorite search engine to look for volunteer opportunities in your area. List 3 things you could volunteer to do.

_____

_____

_____

Practice Test

DIRECTIONS: Read the business letter below to answer the next 4 questions. Use the Answer Sheet.

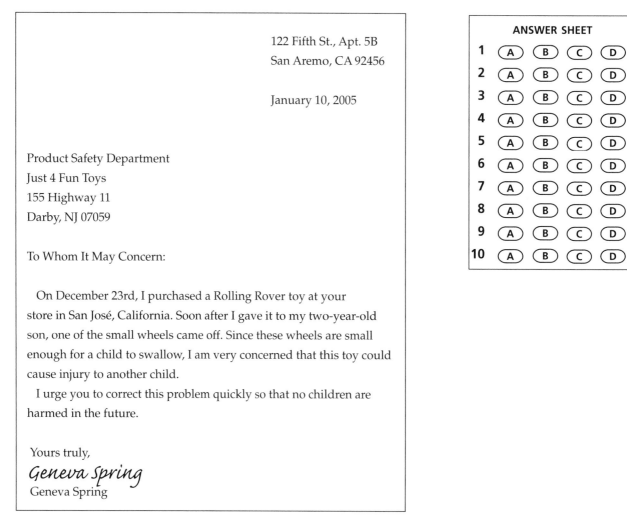

122 Fifth St., Apt. 5B
San Aremo, CA 92456

January 10, 2005

Product Safety Department
Just 4 Fun Toys
155 Highway 11
Darby, NJ 07059

To Whom It May Concern:

   On December 23rd, I purchased a Rolling Rover toy at your store in San José, California. Soon after I gave it to my two-year-old son, one of the small wheels came off. Since these wheels are small enough for a child to swallow, I am very concerned that this toy could cause injury to another child.
   I urge you to correct this problem quickly so that no children are harmed in the future.

Yours truly,

Geneva Spring
Geneva Spring

ANSWER SHEET

1 (A) (B) (C) (D)
2 (A) (B) (C) (D)
3 (A) (B) (C) (D)
4 (A) (B) (C) (D)
5 (A) (B) (C) (D)
6 (A) (B) (C) (D)
7 (A) (B) (C) (D)
8 (A) (B) (C) (D)
9 (A) (B) (C) (D)
10 (A) (B) (C) (D)

1. What was the writer's purpose for writing this letter?

A. to thank someone for something
B. to ask a question
C. to ask for money
D. to report a problem

2. Where is the writer's address?

A. on the upper right side
B. on the upper left side
C. on the lower left side
D. on the lower right side

3. What other salutation could you use for a business letter?

A. Yours truly,
B. Hi
C. Dear Sir / Madam
D. Your friend,

4. Where did the writer sign the letter?

A. below the heading
B. above the closing
C. below the closing
D. above the salutation

DIRECTIONS: Read the job interview tips to answer the next 6 questions. Use the Answer Sheet on page 16.

JOB INTERVIEW TIPS

1) Leave extra time to get to a job interview. It's important that you arrive a few minutes before the interview is supposed to begin.
2) Make sure your appearance is neat and dress appropriately. It's usually better to be overdressed than underdressed.
3) Try not to appear nervous during the interview. Avoid nervous habits such as chewing gum and playing with things in your hand.
4) Speak clearly and concisely and always tell the truth.
5) Make eye contact with the interviewer and speak confidently.
6) Focus on what you can do for the company. Wait until you have been offered the job to ask about the salary and benefits.
7) Use examples from your work and educational background to show that you are hard working, honest, responsible, and a team player.
8) At the end of the interview, shake hands and thank the interviewer for his or her time. You can also say that you are looking forward to hearing from him or her.

5. According to the article, when should you arrive at a job interview?

A. exactly on time
B. a half hour early
C. a little early
D. a little late

6. According to the article, what is one sign of nervousness?

A. looking around
B. playing with things in your hand
C. making eye contact
D. arriving early

7. Which example would show you are a hard worker?

A. I grew up on a farm.
B. I like to get up early in the morning.
C. In addition to my job, I am taking two evening courses.
D. I think I'm a hard worker.

8. Which of these things shouldn't you do at a job interview?

A. speak clearly
B. look directly at the interviewer
C. ask first about the job benefits
D. dress neatly

9. What could you say to show that you are a team player?

A. I enjoy working on group projects.
B. I have a big family.
C. I like team sports.
D. I like to meet new people.

10. Which sentence would be appropriate for you to say at the end of a job interview?

A. When will I hear from you?
B. I hope you don't interview anyone else.
C. I'll call you tomorrow.
D. Thank you for your time.

HOW DID YOU DO? Count the number of correct answers on your answer sheet. Record this number in the bar graph on the inside back cover.

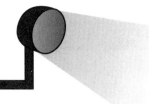

Spotlight: Reading

A What can you infer from each sentence below? Check (✓) the logical inferences.

1. My friend Ted always does his share of the work.

   ❏ Ted is friendly.   ❏ Ted isn't lazy.   ❏ Ted is the hardest worker.

2. Julia never makes any spelling or grammar mistakes when she writes in English.

   ❏ Julia speaks only English.   ❏ Julia is an accurate writer.   ❏ Julia loves to write.

3. Daniela got a promotion even though she has only worked there for a year.

   ❏ Daniela is a good employee.   ❏ Daniela asked for a promotion.   ❏ Daniela plans to quit soon.

4. When Manuel was sick, a lot of people came to visit him.

   ❏ Manuel took a lot of sick days.   ❏ Manuel has a lot of friends.   ❏ Manuel was sick for a long time.

5. Paul didn't answer a lot of the questions on the test because he couldn't concentrate.

   ❏ Paul is a difficult student.   ❏ Paul didn't want to take the test.   ❏ Paul didn't do well on the test.

6. Akiko always speaks softly when she talks on her cell phone in public places.

   ❏ Akiko is polite.   ❏ Akiko doesn't like to talk on the phone.   ❏ Akiko has a cheap phone.

B Study the picture. List 3 facts about the people in the picture. Then make 3 inferences using the information in the picture.

FACTS

1. _____

2. _____

3. _____

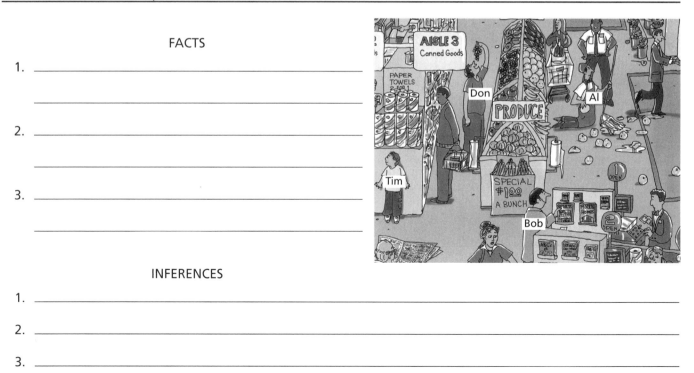

INFERENCES

1. _____

2. _____

3. _____

C Read the article and answer the questions below.

Talent in Two Languages Can Boost Your Career Value

by Deborah Willoughby

When Spanish-speaking people come into Montgomery County, Alabama's Probate Office to renew their car tags[1], many ask for Christie Vazquez.

"They feel more comfortable with people who speak their language," said Vazquez, a clerk who is fluent in Spanish. Vazquez often is called on to help communicate with Spanish-speaking customers throughout the probate department.

As the country becomes more diverse[2], businesses are responding to a greater number of people, both employees and customers, who don't speak English. Learning another language may not be the easiest career-development move[3], but it may be among the most useful.

"Folks who are bilingual are going to be much more employable than those who speak just one language," said Walt Hines who teaches introductory Spanish at a Montgomery, Alabama technical college.

----

[1] tags: car license plates

[2] diverse: varied

[3] career-development move: thing you can do to build your career

1. What skill does Christie Vazquez have that her coworkers don't have?

   _____

2. Why is there a growing need for employees who speak two languages?

   _____

3. Why is learning another language a useful career-development move?

   _____

4. What is Walt Hines' profession?

   _____

5. What can you infer from the information in the article? Check (✓) your answers.

   ❑ Christie Vazquez grew up in Mexico.

   ❑ Christie Vazquez has worked at the probate office for many years.

   ❑ A number of Spanish-speaking people live in Montgomery County, Alabama.

   ❑ Vazquez is bilingual.

   ❑ Walt Hines in a native Spanish speaker.

   ❑ Walt Hines speaks some Spanish.

Spotlight: Writing

A Choose the correct words to complete the descriptions of the parts of a business letter.

| heading | salutation | body |
| inside address | signature | closing |

1. The word "Sincerely" is a common _____ for a business letter.

2. The sender's address is included in the _____.

3. You should handwrite your _____ rather than typing or printing it.

4. The _____ of a letter is the main part.

5. The date is part of the _____.

6. The receiver's address is in the _____.

7. "Dear Sir / Madam" is an example of a _____.

B Use the information on the envelope to complete the letter below.

Ray Jones
245 Harvey Street
Cincinnati, OH 45201

Mr. Ian Talbot
Service Manager
Cablex, Inc.
3459 Andrews Street
Cincinnati, OH 45203

February 18, 2006

Dear

I have been a customer of Cablex since June 2001. At first I was very happy with the service that Cablex provided. Recently, however, I have been having problems with my cable connection and although I have tried several times, I have been unable to get the problem fixed.

Because of this problem, I would like to discontinue the service as of March 1, 2006. Please send a final bill to my mailing address.

Sincerely,

Ray Jones

20

C Add a date, a salutation, and a closing to the letter below.

43 Highland Avenue
Patterson, NJ 07052

Mr. James Darcy
Manager, Shopper's World
432 Winston Avenue
Patterson, NJ 07052

   On October 12, I ordered a pair of binoculars from your store. Today, however, I received a package from your store with a set of pots and pans (which I didn't order) and no binoculars. I am returning the set of pots and pans and I ask that you send out my original order as soon as possible. If you have any questions, please call me at 555-6994.

Elizabeth Bennett
Elizabeth Bennett

D Answer these questions about the business letter in Activity C.

1. Who is the writer of this letter?

_____

2. What does the writer want?

_____

3. What did the writer get that she didn't want?

_____

4. Why did the writer include her telephone number?

_____

5. Do you think this letter is very concise, somewhat concise, or not concise? Why?

_____

6. Do you think this letter is very clear, somewhat clear, or not clear? Why?

_____

LESSON 1

It happened during rush hour.

A Rewrite the direct questions below as indirect questions. Then answer them using information from the picture.

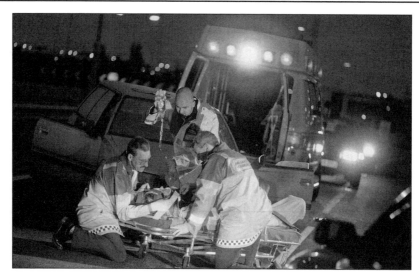

1. What caused the car accident?

   Indirect question: _Do you know what caused the accident?_

   Answer: _____

2. What time of day did the accident happen?

   Indirect question: _____?

   Answer: _____.

3. Was the car damaged?

   Indirect question: _____?

   Answer: _____.

4. Did anyone get hurt?

   Indirect question: _____?

   Answer: _____.

5. Did an ambulance come?

   Indirect question: _____?

   Answer: _____.

6. How many people were in the car?

   Indirect question: _____?

   Answer: _____.

B What can you infer from each statement below? More than 1 answer is possible.

1. Tom always drives very fast.

    You can infer that _____

2. Ken owns his own landscaping company.

    You can infer that _____

3. Sylvia is a police officer.

    You can infer that _____

4. Tito's car broke down on his way to work.

    You can infer that _____

5. Sue bought a motorcycle instead of a car.

    You can infer that _____

C What would you do? Complete the sentences below.

1. If I saw a car accident on the highway, I _____

2. If I rode a motorcycle to work everyday, I _____

3. If I got stopped for speeding, I _____

4. If I could afford to buy a new car, I _____

5. If I could walk to work, I _____

6. If we didn't have road signs on highways, it _____

7. If there weren't any driving laws, _____

8. If fewer people had cars, _____

★★★

TAKE IT OUTSIDE: Talk to 3 friends or classmates. Ask the questions below and complete the chart.

Name	Where did you go yesterday?	How did you get there?	How long did it take?	What problems did you have getting there?

★★★

2 LESSON

My insurance will cover it.

A Match the words that are similar in meaning. Write the words on the lines.

1. incredibly _____   a. include

2. cover _____   b. subtract

3. collide _____   c. ask for

4. deduct _____   d. price

5. amount _____   e. necessary

6. cost _____   f. correct

7. request _____   g. very; extremely

8. essential _____   h. damage

9. accurate _____   i. quantity

                                              j. hit

B Add the missing noun and verb forms to the chart. Use the correct form of each word in the questions below. Then answer the questions.

NOUNS	VERBS
1.	collide
2. payment	
3.	insure
4. agreement	
5. depreciation	
6. coverage	
7. injury	

1. What might cause two cars to _____?

_____

2. What monthly _____ do you make?

_____

3. Do you have health _____?

_____

4. What are you and your friends usually in _____ about?

_____

24

5. Why do cars in cold climates _____ faster than cars in warm climates?

   _____

6. Does your insurance _____ your personal possessions?

   _____

7. What can people do to reduce their chance of _____ in a car accident?

   _____

C Add the missing words to the sentences below.

claim	comprehensive	medical	policy
collision	liability	uninsured motorist	premium

1. The _____ is the amount of money you pay for your insurance.

2. The contract between the driver and the insurance company is called a _____.

3. If you hit a wall or some other object, your _____ coverage will pay for the damage to your car.

4. If your car is stolen, your _____ coverage will pay for the loss.

5. It's important to have _____ insurance if you injure someone else in a car accident.

6. _____ insurance helps to pay medical expenses for the driver of the policy holder's car and any passengers.

7. If you want to collect insurance money after an accident, you have to file a _____.

8. If your car is hit by someone without car insurance, _____ insurance will help to pay for injuries to the people in your car.

D Match each situation to a type of coverage.

liability	collision	comprehensive	medical	uninsured motorist

1. Ian lost control of his car and hit a tree. Ian wasn't hurt but the front end of his car was damaged. What type of coverage will pay for the damage to his car? _____

2. Keiko fell asleep while driving and her car went off the road. Keiko wasn't hurt but her sister Ayako broke her arm. What type of coverage will pay for Ayako's medical expenses? _____

3. Imad suffered minor injuries when another car drove through a red light and hit his car. The other driver did not have car insurance. What coverage could pay for his injuries? _____

 TAKE IT ONLINE: Use your favorite search engine to look up the Kelley Blue Book price of a car you would like to own.

Could you tell me the arrival time?

3
LESSON

A Number each conversation in order starting with #1.

Conversation A

_____ We sure do.

_____ A ticket to Andover, please.

_____ Gate 12. And that will be $56.00.

_____ Round trip or one way?

_____ Hmm, let's see. The next bus leaves in thirty-five minutes.

__1__ Next, please.

_____ What gate does it leave from?

_____ Do you take credit cards?

_____ Round trip, please. And could you tell me when the next bus is?

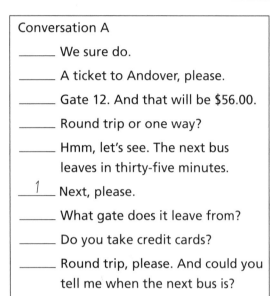

Conversation B

_____ I need a one-way ticket to Frankville.

_____ Thanks.

_____ Yes, that's right.

_____ Sure.

__1__ What can I do for you?

_____ Okay. That comes to $15.75.

_____ Did you say Frankville?

_____ Do you have change for a fifty?

B Use the bus schedule to decide if the statements below are true or false. Circle your answer.

1. A bus leaves Danville for Hinsdale every hour between 5 in the morning and 8 at night. TRUE FALSE

2. The first bus in the morning leaves Saco at 5:00. TRUE FALSE

3. It takes the 5 A.M. bus an hour and a half to get from Danville to Hinsdale. TRUE FALSE

4. Saco is closer to Danville than Hinsdale. TRUE FALSE

5. There are more buses to Hinsdale in the morning than in the afternoon. TRUE FALSE

6. The first bus to leave Danville in the afternoon arrives in Hinsdale at 3:30. TRUE FALSE

7. There are two express buses from Danville to Hinsdale. TRUE FALSE

8. The 7 A.M. bus from Danville arrives in Saco at 7:30 A.M. TRUE FALSE

BUS SCHEDULE		
Leave Danville	**Leave Saco**	**Arrive Hinsdale**
05:00A	05:30A	06:30A
06:00A	06:30A	07:30A
07:00A	—	08:10A
08:00A	—	09:10A
09:00A	09:30A	10:30A
11:00A	11:30A	12:30P
01:00P	01:30P	02:30P
03:00P	03:30P	03:30P
06:00P	06:30P	07:30P
10:00P	10:30P	11:30P

C Read the flight information and answer the questions below.

FLIGHT SCHEDULE ✈

Select Your Departing Flight for Fri., Sept. 1, 2006

Price	Departing	Arriving	Travel Time	Flight Number
$242.00	1:55 P.M. New York, NY (LGA)	3:07 P.M. Philadelphia, PA (PHL)	1hr 12min	321
	Change Planes. Connect time in Philadelphia, PA (PHL) is 3 hours 3 minutes.			
	6:10 P.M. Philadelphia, PA (PHL)	9:13 P.M. Miami, FL (MIA)	3hr 3min	265
$195.00 Non-stop	2:22 P.M. New York, NY (LGA)	5:26 P.M. Miami, FL (MIA)	3hr 4min	488
$517.30	6:40 A.M. New York, NY (LGA)	8:18 A.M. Cleveland, OH (CLE)	1hr 38min	544
	Change Planes. Connect time in Cleveland, OH (CLE) is 1 hour 2 minutes.			
	9:20 A.M. Cleveland, OH (CLE)	12:11 P.M. Miami, FL (MIA)	2hr 51min	299

1. Which flight or flights take the most time to get from New York to Miami? _____

2. Which flight or flights take the least time to get from New York to Miami? _____

3. Which flight or flights has the longer layover between connecting flights? _____

4. Which flight is the least expensive? _____

5. Which flight or flights are the best deal? Why?

_____

D Complete these conversations using the flight information above.

1. A: Can you tell me when flight 488 leaves New York?

   B: Yes. It leaves New York at _____

2. A: Can you tell me when flight 299 arrives in Miami?

   B: _____

3. A: Can you tell me how long the flight between Philadelphia and Miami is?

   B: _____

4. A: Do you know how long the layover in Cleveland is?

   B: _____

Planning a Trip

A Use the time zone map to answer the questions below.

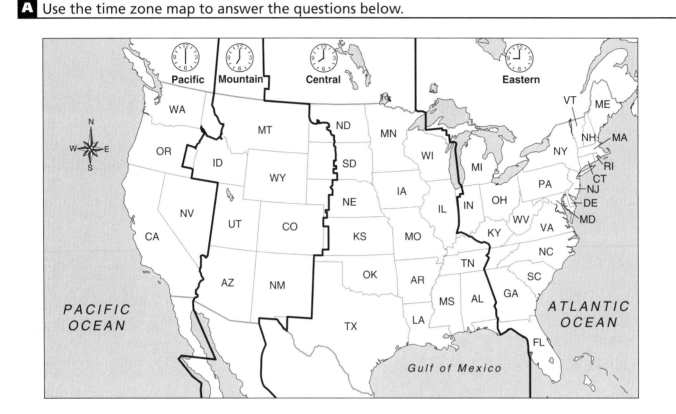

1. How many different time zones are there in the continental United States? _____

2. When it is noon in New York, what time is it in California? _____

3. When it is midnight in Florida, what time is it in Iowa? _____

4. When it is 3 P.M. in New Mexico, what time is it in New York? _____

5. When it is midnight in Arizona, what time is it in Colorado? _____

6. If your plane left New York at noon and your flight to Los Angeles was 6 hours long, what time would it

   be in Los Angeles when you arrived? _____

   What time would it be in New York when you arrived in Los Angeles? _____

7. Your flight left New York at 9 A.M. (EST) and arrived in New Mexico at noon (Mountain Time).

   How long was your flight? _____

8. Your flight left Oregon at 10 in the morning and it took 8 hours to get to Miami. What time was it in

   Miami when you arrived? _____

28

B Use the highway map to answer the questions below.

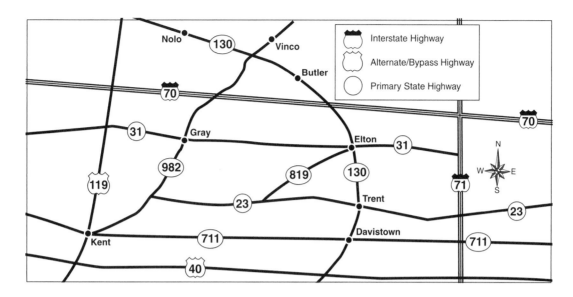

1. According to the map, which interstate highway goes north/south?

   A. Rt. 31   B. Rt. 70   C. Rt. 71   D. Rt. 130

2. Which road runs parallel to Rt. 711?

   A. Rt. 119   B. Rt. 40   C. Rt. 819   D. Rt. 982

3. Which town is directly north of Gray?

   A. Nolo   B. Elton   C. Kent   D. Trent

4. Which is the shortest route from Kent to Elton?

   A. Rt. 711 to 130 B. Rt. 119 to 31   C. Rt. 982 to 23 to 819   D. Rt. 982 to 70 to 130

5. Which road connects Davistown and Trent?

   A. Interstate 71   B. Rt. 119   C. Rt. 130   D. Rt 711

6. Which road is an interstate highway?

   A. 23   B. 71   C. 819   D. 119

C Use the map above to complete these directions. Write *east, west, north,* or *south.*

1. To get from Gray to Elton you should go _____ on Route 31.

2. To get from Elton to Butler, you should go _____ on Route 130.

3. You can take Route 982 _____ to go from Kent to Gray.

4. The shortest way from Trent to Kent is to take 23 _____ and 982

   _____ .

5. To get from Butler to Interstate 71, just go _____ on 130 until you reach Interstate 70.

   Then go _____ on 70 until you hit Interstate 71.

5 LESSON

I should have stayed home.

A Complete the sentences with *should have* or *shouldn't have*.

1. Jamal missed his flight because he got stuck in traffic and was late to the airport. I guess he _____ left home earlier.

2. I didn't see the car behind me and I backed into it. I guess I _____ looked behind more carefully.

3. I felt sick at work all day today. I guess I _____ gone to work. I _____ stayed home.

4. Juan had to pay a lot for his plane ticket because he didn't buy it until two days before the flight. Now he knows he _____ bought it at least two weeks before the flight.

5. The airlines lost Sandra's luggage so for three days she didn't have any clean clothes to wear. Now she knows she _____ put some clothes in her carry-on bag.

6. Ali _____ taken Route 90 because there's always a traffic jam during rush hour.

B Answer the questions below about the world's worst driver.

1. When Tony saw the stop sign, he ignored it. What should he have done?

_____

2. When Tony saw the blinking yellow light, he sped up. What should he have done?

_____

3. When Tony saw the blinking red light, he slowed down a little. What should he have done?

_____

4. When Tony saw pedestrians in the crosswalk, he didn't stop. What should he have done?

_____

5. When Tony heard an ambulance behind him, he didn't move his car over. What should he have done?

_____

C Study the photographs and answer the questions.

1. Samantha got ketchup on her white shirt. What could she have done to avoid this? List 3 things.

   • *She could have* _____

   • _____

   _____

   • _____

   _____

2. What do you think she should have done?

   _____

   _____

3. Chan got wet while he was waiting for the bus to arrive. What could he have done to avoid this? List 3 things.

   • _____

   • _____

   • _____

4. What do you think he should have done?

   _____

   _____

UNIT 2: Getting Around

FAMILY LESSON

What's there to do?

A Read the Calendar of Events and circle the 3 most interesting activities. Then write a sentence telling why each activity is interesting to you.

EXAMPLE: *I'm interested in the Summer Insects program because it's free and my children like to do things outdoors.*

1. _____

   _____

2. _____

   _____

3. _____

   _____

CALENDAR OF EVENTS

Concerts

Bradford Elementary School, Bradford – "Wayne from Maine," family concert, Saturday, 1 P.M. $6/adults, $4/kids. Info: 555-3838.

Glendale Community Music School, Glendale – Youth Symphony Orchestra, Saturday, 7 P.M. Info: 555-8839.

Palace Theater, Glendale – Palace Youth Theater presents "Schoolhouse Rock, Live" at 7 P.M. Friday and 10 A.M. Saturday. Info: 555-9088.

Theater

Glendale High School, Glendale – The King and I, Friday, 7 P.M. free. Info: 555-4394.

Saint Anselm College, Bradford – The Tamborines, folk dancers, Saturday, 8 P.M., Dana Center. Info: 555-3030.

Town Hall, Bradford – Weekend Family Series begins at 2 P.M. on Sunday. Circle Comedy Clowns. Tickets are $5. Info: 555-2142.

Speakers

Glendale Town Hall, Glendale – "An Afternoon of Humor," with Sandra Hale, Sunday, 2 P.M. Info: 555-3383.

Books

Turner Bookstore, Glendale – Storytime, Saturday, 11 A.M. Info: 555-3993.

Glendale Public Library, Glendale – "Lapsit," stories, rhymes, and songs, through age 2, Fridays, 10 A.M. "Books at Bedtime," story program for all ages, Fridays, 7 P.M. Free programs. Info: 555-4993.

Outdoors

Glendale Nature Center, Glendale – "Summer Insects," family program, Sunday, 1:30 P.M. Free. Registration required. Info: 555-4753.

Silk Farm, Bradford – For kids/families, "The Masked Bandit," Saturday, 9:30–11 A.M. Program for preschoolers and an accompanying adult. $3/$5, Registration required. Info: 555-7798.

B Use the information in the Calendar of Events in Activity A to answer the questions below.

1. How many of the activities are free? _____

2. How many of the activities require registration?

   _____

3. How many of the activities are especially for children and families? _____

4. If a family of 2 adults and 3 children wanted to go to the program at the Silk Farm in Bradford, how much would it cost? _____

5. A family of 6 (two adults and four children ages 6, 8, 9, and 11) is looking for something to do on Saturday. Which program would you recommend? Why?

_____

_____

C The activities in the calendar on page 32 are organized by type. Reorganize them by day of the week.

Activities on Friday	Activities on Saturday	Activities on Sunday
Schoolhouse Rock, Live	Wayne from Maine family concert	

★ ★

TAKE IT OUTSIDE: Look in local newspapers to find listings of events in your area. Bring the listings to class and share what you learned.

★ ★

TAKE IT ONLINE: Most public libraries offer free activities for both children and adults. Many libraries also have free passes to museums and other special places in the area. Use your favorite search engine to find the website of a public library in your area. Look at the library's calendar of events to find out what is happening this month. Report what you learned to your classmates.

WORK

LESSON

Can you tell me how to get there?

A Study the map below and circle the answer that best completes each sentence.

1. Trenton is _____ of Mercerville.
   A. northwest
   B. southeast
   C. southwest

2. Penn Valley is directly _____ of Sylvan Glen.
   A. east
   B. north
   C. west

3. Mercerville is _____ of Morrisville.
   A. northeast
   B. northwest
   C. southeast

4. Route 295 runs parallel to Route _____.
   A. 1
   B. 195
   C. 29

5. Route 29 crosses Route _____.
   A. 13
   B. 195
   C. 1

6. Route 29 becomes Route _____.
   A. 1
   B. 295
   C. 195

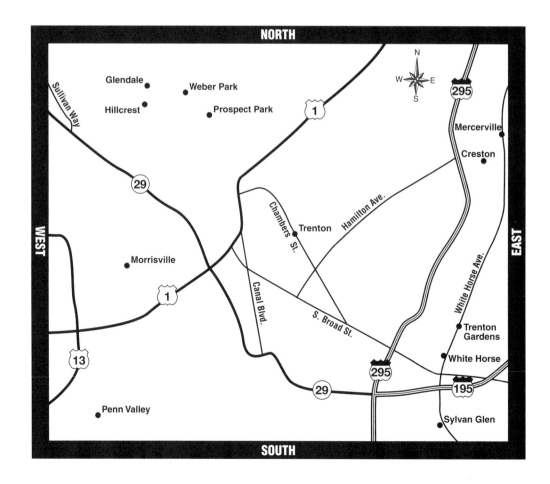

B Read each situation below. Then use the map on page 34 to complete the directions to each place of work. Circle the correct answer.

1. Situation: You work at a store on the northeast corner of Canal Blvd. and S. Broad St. A customer wants directions to the store from the intersection of Route 13 and Route 1.

   Directions: Go _____ (north/south) on Route 1. When you get to S. Broad St. turn _____ (right/left). The store is on the _____ (left/right) side of S. Broad Street.

2. Situation: Your office is on the northeastern side of Sullivan Way. A salesperson asks you for directions to your office from Creston.

   Directions: Get onto Route 295 going _____ (north/south/east/west). Continue on 295 until you get to _____ (Route 1/Route 29). Go _____ (east/west). After _____ (Route 1/Route 13) look for the exit for Sullivan Way. The office is about a mile up on the right side of Sullivan Way.

3. Situation: A truck driver needs to get to your place of business in Trenton Gardens. He calls you on his cell phone and says that he is in Penn Valley right now.

   Directions: You want to get on Route 13 going _____ (north/south). When you get to Route _____ (1/29), go north. Stay on this road until you get to Route 29 where you want to go _____ (east/west). After Route 29 crosses Route 295, it becomes Route _____ (13/195). Stay on this road until you see the sign for White Horse Avenue. Go _____ (north/south) on White Horse until you come to Trenton Gardens. The company is on the right on White Horse Avenue.

C Write the directions from Sylvan Glen to your place of work in Weber Park.

_____

_____

_____

_____

_____

_____

★★★

TAKE IT OUTSIDE: Interview a classmate. Find out the person's home or work address and ask for directions from their home or work to your school.

★★★

TAKE IT ONLINE: Use your favorite search engine to look for a map of your area. Request directions from your classmate's home or work to your school. Then compare the online directions with your classmate's directions.

Practice Test

DIRECTIONS: Read the insurance bill to answer the next 4 questions. Use the Answer Sheet.

Bob Jones Automobile Insurance Co.
4695 Breyer Road
San Antonio, Texas 78288

STATEMENT

Payment DUE DATE 10-01-05

TO CHANGE A POLICY, CALL
1-800-555-3594
FOR BILLING QUESTIONS, CALL
1-800-467-9377
TO REPORT A CLAIM, CALL
1-800-569-5699

VICTOR DANKO
552 MONTEREY BLVD.
SAN ANTONIO, TX 78201

POLICY PERIOD
OCT-01-05 TO APR-01-06

DESCRIBED VEHICLE

MAKE	YEAR	BODY STYLE	VEHICLE IDENTIFICATION NUMBER	PREMIUM FOR THIS POLICY PERIOD
MAZDA	2002	4DR	3B356AW49499	$286.80

---

1. Who is being insured with this policy?

   A. Bob Jones

   B. Mazda 02

   C. Victor Danko

   D. none of the above

2. When is a payment due?

   A. October 10, 2006

   B. January 10, 2005

   C. October 1, 2005

   D. April 1, 2006

3. How long is this policy in effect?

   A. one month

   B. six months

   C. one year

   D. two years

4. What is the annual premium for this policy?

   A. $28.60

   B. $286.80

   C. $573.60

   D. $858.40

ANSWER SHEET

1 (A) (B) (C) (D)
2 (A) (B) (C) (D)
3 (A) (B) (C) (D)
4 (A) (B) (C) (D)
5 (A) (B) (C) (D)
6 (A) (B) (C) (D)
7 (A) (B) (C) (D)
8 (A) (B) (C) (D)
9 (A) (B) (C) (D)
10 (A) (B) (C) (D)

DIRECTIONS: Read the information about reporting an accident to answer the next 6 questions. Use the Answer Sheet on page 36.

When you are required to report an accident to DMV

If you are involved in a vehicle accident that occurred in California, you must report it to DMV if:
• there was property damage of more than $750 **or**
• anyone was injured (no matter how minor) **or** killed.

Each driver must make a report to DMV within 10 days, whether you caused the accident or not, and even if the accident occurred on private property.

You must complete a DMV Traffic Accident Report form SR 1/SR 1A.

When you have completed the form, you can mail it to:
      Department of Motor Vehicles
      Financial Responsibility (Mail Station J-237)
      PO Box 942884
      Sacramento, California 94284-0884

If you do not submit this report, your driving privilege will be suspended. DMV may ask your insurance company to verify that you had coverage in effect at the time of the accident. If you did not have insurance, your driving privilege will be suspended for one year. To get your license back, after the suspension, you will need to provide proof of financial responsibility and maintain it on record for three years. The accident may count as one point on your driving record (California Insurance Requirements).

Source: http://www.dmv.ca.gov/

---

5. Who do these instructions apply to?
  A. California residents only
  B. anyone who is driving in California
  C. California residents over the age of 70
  D. all uninsured motorists

6. Which of the following topics is not included in the instructions for reporting an accident?
  A. who needs to report an accident
  B. how long you have to report an accident
  C. what happens after you report the accident
  D. what happens if you don't report the accident

7. According to the article above, when don't you have to report an accident?
  A. when no one was hurt seriously
  B. when no one was injured and damages were $750 or less
  C. when there was no one in the other car
  D. when you are a resident of a state other than California

8. According to the article above, which of the following statements is true?
  A. You don't have to file an accident report if there was no damage and no one was hurt.
  B. You don't have to file a report if the accident took place on your driveway.
  C. You have to pay a fine if you send your report late.
  D. You have two weeks to report an accident.

9. According to the article above, which of the following statements is true?
  A. You should report an accident by calling the Department of Motor Vehicles.
  B. Only the driver who caused the accident should file a report.
  C. If you don't have insurance, you will lose your driver's license for a month.
  D. You have ten days to report an accident.

10. What form should you use to report an accident in California?
  A. Form J-237   C. Form SR /
  B. Form 94284   D. Form SR 1/SR 1A

HOW DID YOU DO? Count the number of correct answers on your answer sheet. Record this number in the bar graph on the inside back cover.

Spotlight: Reading

A Read each paragraph below and identify the topic and the main idea.

1

The last trip I took was in 2003. That year I went to Italy to visit my brother. I thought this would be a great trip, but in fact, it was pretty awful. The worst thing that happened was that my brother got the flu and he had to stay in bed the whole time I was there. Besides that, the airlines lost my luggage on the flight over so for the first three days of my trip, I didn't have any clean clothes to put on. And then, to top it off, it rained every day I was there.

Topic: _____

Main Idea: _____

_____

_____

_____

2

Yesterday a car pulled into the road right in front of me. The driver was talking on his cell phone and he never even saw me. It was only because I stepped on the brake that I was able to avoid an accident. Another time I was driving on the highway and a car passed me going quite fast. When I looked at the driver, I noticed that he was shaving his face! It's amazing the stupid things people will do while they are driving.

Topic: _____

Main Idea: _____

_____

_____

_____

3

There are many different ways to get around in the United States. Many cities have buses, trains (or "subways"), trolleys, or streetcars. For a small fee, you can ride these vehicles. In some places, you can buy a card good for several trips on subways or buses. You can also pay for each trip separately. Taxicabs, or "taxis," are cars that take you where you want to go for a fee. Taxis are more expensive than other types of public transportation.

Topic: _____

Main Idea: _____

_____

_____

_____

4

Owning a car is a convenient way to get around but it's expensive too. In addition to paying for the car, you have to pay for car insurance and registration. You also have to pay for car maintenance and repairs. And don't forget the cost of gasoline, parking, and tolls. It's important to think of all the costs before you decide to buy a car.

Topic: _____

Main Idea: _____

_____

_____

_____

B Read the article. What is the topic and main idea of each paragraph? Write your answers in the chart below.

Save Money on Gasoline

1   Do you wish you could spend less money on gasoline for your automobile? You can. All you have to do is follow a few simple rules of car ownership.

2   One of the easiest ways to save money on gasoline is just to change the way you drive. If you drive fewer miles, you will spend less on gasoline. However, if this isn't possible, you can also reduce the amount of money you spend on gasoline by driving more slowly. By reducing your speed just 5 to 10 miles per hour below the speed limit, you could improve your fuel efficiency by 10%. That translates into a substantial savings.

3   Checking the air pressure in your tires can make a difference in fuel efficiency. Tires lose pressure over time, forcing the engine of the car to work harder to push the vehicle forward. That translates into lower gas mileage and more money spent on gasoline. Check your tire pressure regularly and you will save money on gasoline.

4   Keeping your car in good condition with regular tune-ups can also help you save money on gasoline. For example, regularly changing the fuel filter prevents dirt from collecting in the fuel tank. This can help you to get the best possible gas mileage.

5   You can also save money on gas by improving the aerodynamics of your car. Roof racks, for example, create air turbulence which decreases fuel efficiency. Carrying heavy things in your car will do the same.

6   Another way to save money on gasoline is to pay attention to when you fill up the tank. Most people wait until their gas tank is almost empty before they fill it up again. However, this can cause dirt in the tank to pass into the fuel filter. You might get better gas mileage if you refill the gas tank when it still has a quarter of a tank of gas.

Paragraph	Topic	Main Idea
1		
2		
3		
4		
5		
6		

Spotlight: Writing

A Add information from the box to each sentence below.

Nouns		Verbs
snow	signals	speeding
bumpers	car safety seats	direct traffic
liability	ambulance	register
driver's license	driving test	

1. Cars have to have a windshield.

   Cars have to have a windshield and bumpers.

2. You can get a traffic ticket for parking illegally.

   _____

3. Police officers help in emergencies.

   _____

4. You should drive extra carefully in fog.

   _____

5. It's important to have collision coverage.

   _____

6. You should obey all traffic laws.

   _____

7. Pull over to the side of the road if a police car wants to pass you.

   _____

8. You must take a vision test before you can get a driver's license.

   _____

9. If you own a car, you have to pay to insure it.

   _____

10. Your insurance card must be with you whenever you drive.

   _____

B Combine each pair of sentences, using *and* or *but*.

1. Karla doesn't have a driver's license yet. She is taking driving lessons now.

   _____

2. Joel can afford to buy a car. He can't afford to pay for car insurance.

   _____

3. You should change the oil in your car regularly. You should keep your tires properly inflated.

   _____

4. You should obey the speed limit. You should always wear your seatbelt.

   _____

5. You can rent a car instead of buying one. It's expensive to rent a car.

   _____

6. You can get a cheap flight if you are willing to make several stops. It can take a long time to get to your destination.

   _____

7. It's convenient to own a car. It's expensive to own a car.

   _____

8. You can buy a new car. A new car depreciates quickly.

   _____

C Rewrite the body of the letter below. Make the writing smoother by combining sentences.

September 12, 2006

Dear Sam,

   I want you to know that I feel terrible about the damage done to your car. I want to take full responsibility for repairing it.
   It was very thoughtful of you to say it was minor damage. I won't feel good until it is fixed. I hope you won't mind that I called Dan's Garage. I asked them to look at the damage and give an estimate.
   Please accept my apologies. I hope this will not affect our friendship.

   My best,

   Josh

LESSON 1

Call 911!

A Write the past tense of each verb below.

1. take _____
2. feel _____
3. fall _____
4. arrive _____
5. ride _____
6. give _____

7. run _____
8. pass out _____
9. bring _____
10. see _____
11. say _____
12. get _____

B Combine the information in each pair of sentences with *and* or *but*.

1. Oscar was at home when he got sick. His wife was there too.

   _____

2. Oscar tried to stand up. He fell to the floor.

   _____

3. Oscar's wife ran to the phone. She quickly called 911.

   _____

4. An ambulance rushed to Oscar's house. Oscar didn't want to go to the hospital.

   _____

5. The EMTs put Oscar in the ambulance. They put an oxygen mask on his face.

   _____

6. Oscar rode to the hospital in the back of the ambulance. His wife followed in their car.

   _____

7. A doctor gave Oscar some medicine. A nurse took his vital signs.

   _____

8. Oscar wanted to leave the hospital. The doctor said he should stay there for several days.

   _____

9. There was plenty of food to eat at the hospital. Oscar wasn't very hungry.

   _____

10. After a week, Oscar felt much better. The doctors said he could go home.

    _____

C Read the information and answer the questions below.

When Should You Go to the Emergency Room?

At 7 in the morning, Ted suddenly felt a squeezing pain in the center of his chest. The pain then spread to his shoulders, neck, and arms. Ted thought he was going to faint, so he called to his wife, Nancy. Nancy wanted to call for an ambulance, but Ted asked her to wait awhile. Thirty minutes later, Ted didn't feel any better, so he asked Nancy to drive him to the hospital. By the time they arrived at the hospital, Ted was having trouble breathing. By the time Nancy stopped the car at the entrance to the emergency room, Ted was having a major heart attack. Nancy says she wishes she had called 911 and gotten Ted to the hospital right away, but like most people Ted didn't want to go and Nancy wasn't sure it was an emergency situation.

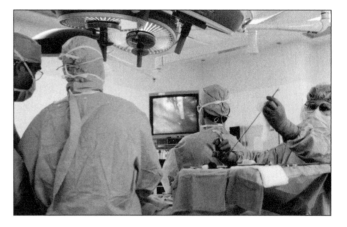

It's not always easy to know when to go to the emergency room, but if you are in doubt, it's always better to be safe than sorry. In most areas, you should dial 911 if you think someone needs emergency help. For some kinds of emergencies, every minute can make the difference between life and death, so don't delay.

If you take someone with a non-life-threatening problem to the emergency room, you can help make sure the patient is taken care of properly. The patient will need to check in with the triage nurse in the emergency room. The triage nurse will assess the patient's condition to determine how serious it is. The patient will also need to provide information about his or her medical history, drug allergies, medications, and health insurance coverage. While you are waiting in the emergency room, you should also watch for any changes in the patient's condition; let the nurse know if the person seems to be getting worse.

1. What were Ted's symptoms?

   _____

   _____

2. What should Nancy have done?

   _____

   _____

3. What does a triage nurse do?

   _____

   _____

4. What information do patients need to provide when they go to the emergency room?

   _____

   _____

2 LESSON

Who's your doctor?

A Complete each sentence with the name of the correct health care professional.

Health Care Professionals

cardiologist	general practitioner	optometrist
dental hygienist	nutritionist	pediatrician
dermatologist	obstetrician	psychiatrist

1. An _____ specializes in eye diseases.

2. If you want to get your teeth cleaned, you can make an appointment with a _____.

3. If you have a rash or itchy skin, you should see a _____.

4. Neither a dental hygienist nor a _____ is a medical doctor.

5. If you have a family history of heart disease, your _____ might refer you to a _____.

6. If your child has an earache, you can take her to a _____.

7. If you lose interest in everything around you, you might want to see a _____.

8. An _____ delivers babies.

B Compare the 2 health care professionals. Add 3 ideas to the Venn Diagram below.

JOB TITLE: Dietician	**JOB TITLE: Physical Therapist**
• Most jobs are in hospitals, nursing care facilities, and offices of physicians or other health practitioners. • Dieticians need at least a bachelor's degree in dietetics, foods, and nutrition or a related area. • Average employment growth is expected.	• About two-thirds of physical therapists work either in hospitals or in private offices. • After graduating from an accredited physical therapist educational program, therapists must pass a licensure exam before they can practice. • Employment is expected to increase faster than the average.

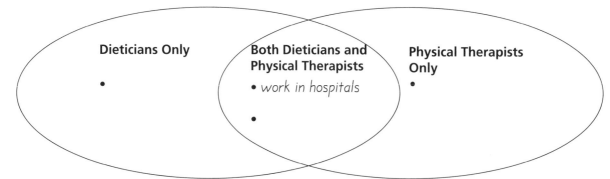

Dieticians Only
•

Both Dieticians and Physical Therapists
• *work in hospitals*
•

Physical Therapists Only
•

C Use the information in the article and your background knowledge to answer the questions below.

Medical Records and Health Information Technicians

Significant Points

- This is one of the few health occupations in which there is little or no direct contact with patients.
- Medical records and health information technicians entering the field usually have an associate degree; courses include anatomy, physiology, medical terminology, and computer science.
- Job prospects should be very good, particularly in offices of physicians.

Nature of the Work

Every time a patient receives health care, a record is maintained of the observations, medical or surgical interventions, and treatment outcomes. This record includes information that the patient provides concerning his or her symptoms and medical history, the results of examinations, reports of x-rays and laboratory tests, diagnoses, and treatment plans. Medical records and health information technicians organize and evaluate these records for completeness and accuracy.

Technicians begin to assemble patients' health information by first making sure their initial medical charts are complete. They ensure that all forms are completed and properly identified and signed, and that all necessary information is in the computer. They regularly communicate with physicians or other health care professionals to clarify diagnoses or to obtain additional information.

Working Conditions

Medical records and health information technicians usually work a 40-hour week. Some overtime may be required. In hospitals—where health information departments are often open 24 hours a day, 7 days a week—technicians may work day, evening, and night shifts.

Medical records and health information technicians work in pleasant and comfortable offices. This is one of the few health occupations in which there is little or no direct contact with patients. Because accuracy is essential in their jobs, technicians must pay close attention to detail. Technicians who work at computer monitors for prolonged periods must guard against eyestrain and muscle pain.

Source: Excerpted from the U.S. government Occupational Handbook

---

1. What are 4 tasks that health information technicians do?

   - _____   • _____
   - _____   • _____

2. What skills do health information technicians need to have? _____

3. Why do health information technicians need to have good communication skills? _____

4. What would you like and dislike about this type of work? Complete the chart below.

Things I would like about the job:	Things I would dislike about the job:
•	•
•	•
•	•

 TAKE IT ONLINE: Use your favorite search engine to find the U.S. Government's Occupational Handbook. Choose a profession in the medical field to read about and list 3 things you would like and dislike about this job.

3 LESSON

That was the 22nd, not the 28th.

A Number each conversation in order starting with #1. Then add the information from the conversations to the appointment calendar below.

Conversation A

_____ Yes, the fifth would work fine.

_____ Yes, I have.

_____ I'm calling to set up an appointment.

_____ Yes. It's 555-9904.

_____ Have you been here before?

_____ I'm sorry, that was the 15th, not the 5th.

_____ Your name please?

_____ Yes, that's right. Can I have your phone number, please?

_____ Could you come in at noon on the 15th, Ms. James?

_____ The 15th? Oh, that's fine too. You said noon?

___1___ Dr. Ray's Office. How can I help you?

_____ It's James. Beverly James.

Conversation B

_____ Okay. Let me look for a morning appointment. What about the 15th at 8:30?

_____ And when would you like to come in?

_____ Yes, this is Chris Ma calling. I need to change an appointment I have with Dr. Ray.

_____ And when is your appointment?

___1___ Dr. Ray's office.

_____ It's this coming Friday at nine.

_____ That would be perfect.

_____ Does she have any openings next week?

_____ No, that won't work. I can only come in the morning.

_____ Let me see. Yes, she has an opening on the 12th at 2. Would you like that?

_____ And your telephone number is 555-8847?

_____ Yes, that's correct.

Conversation C

_____ I think it was 11 o'clock.

_____ What day was your appointment?

_____ Yes, this in Juanita Perez calling. I need to cancel an appointment.

_____ And the time?

_____ It was on the 15th.

_____ Yes, I see it now. Do you want to reschedule that?

___1___ Dr. Ray's office. Can I help you?

_____ Not right now, thank you. I'll call back later.

Appointments Calendar ⊠ ⊟ ⊞

Date: May 15, 2006 ▼ **Doctor:** Ray, Sylvia ▼

Start Time	Patient's Name	Procedure	Home Phone
08:30			
09:00	Oscar Hernandez	Follow-up	555-8574
09:30	Paul Smith	VAC	555-4586
10:00			
10:30	Sara Chang	EXAM	555-4733
11:00	Juanita Perez	Regular Visit	555-9955
11:30			
12:00			
12:30			

B Use the appointments calendar on page 46 to answer the questions below.

1. How many appointments does Dr. Ray now have on the 15th? _____

2. When is Ms. Chang's appointment? _____

3. What is the purpose of Oscar's appointment? _____

4. How much time does Dr. Ray spend with each patient? _____

5. According to this calendar, when will Dr. Ray finish seeing her last patient on the 15th? _____

C Read the medical bill and answer the questions below.

INSURANCE INFORMATION ON FILE
PRIMARY COMPANY NAME

Star Insurance

I.D. # 74976044

CORE PHYSICIANS

BUSINESS HOURS: 8:00 AM TO 4:30 PM
BILLING INQUIRIES: 555-2596

SANDRA CHEN
45 BLAZER DRIVE
ORION, IL 61273

CLOSING DATE 2/07/06

STATEMENT OF PATIENT ACCOUNT
PATIENT'S NAME
Sandra Chen
ACCOUNT NUMBER
TI3594056

MAKE CHECKS PAYABLE TO:
CORE PHYSICIANS
AMOUNT ENCLOSED $ _____
PLEASE WRITE PATIENT ACCOUNT
NUMBER ON CHECK
**MASTERCARD / VISA ACCEPTED
—SEE REVERSE SIDE—**

TO ASSURE PROPER CREDIT TO YOUR ACCOUNT, PLEASE DETACH THIS PORTION AND RETURN WITH YOUR PAYMENT
- -

CORE PHYSICIANS

CPT	ICD.9.CM	DATE	DESCRIPTION	DOCTOR	CHARGES	PAYMENTS/ ADJUSTMENTS	AMOUNT BILLED TO INSURANCE	AMOUNT DUE FROM PATIENT
3500	3445	01/23/06	OFFICE/OP VISIT	GRINEL	90.00		90.00	

ACCOUNT TOTAL	INSURANCE PENDING	AMOUNT NOW DUE	PAY AMOUNT	0.00
90.00	90.00	0.00	NOW DUE ON OR BEFORE	3/07/06

---

1. Which doctor did the patient see? _____

2. This bill is for an appointment that took place on what date? _____

3. Which part of the bill does the patient send back—the top part or the bottom part? _____

4. How much does the patient need to pay now? _____

5. Can patients use credit cards to pay bills from this office? _____

6. If you had a question about this bill, what number would you call? _____

4 LESSON
Food Labels

A Read this information and the statements on page 49. Check (✓) *True* or *False*.

Q: Why are fruits and vegetables important for my health?

A: This year in the United States, more than 1.4 million Americans will be diagnosed with cancer and over 500,000 Americans will die of cancer. An estimated 32% of these deaths may be related to diet. Fruit and vegetable intake is an important part of a healthy diet that may reduce risk of cancer. The health benefits of fruits and vegetables go beyond cancer prevention. During recent decades, studies examining the relationship between dietary patterns and health have found that a diet rich in fruits and vegetables has been associated with the prevention of heart disease, the leading cause of death in the U.S., as well.

Q: How many fruits and vegetables should be eaten daily for good health?

A: The National Academy of Sciences, U.S. Department of Agriculture (USDA), the National Cancer Institute, and the American Cancer Society recommend that 5 to 9 servings of fruits and vegetables be consumed each day depending on a person's energy intake, to reduce risk of cancer and maintain good health. Many adults should be eating closer to 9 daily servings for maximum health benefits!

Source: http://www.cdc.gov/

	True	False
1. More than a million people in the U.S. will learn that they have cancer this year.	☐	☐
2. All deaths from cancer are related to poor diet.	☐	☐
3. Eating fruits and vegetables may help to prevent cancer.	☐	☐
4. Eating a lot of fruit and vegetables will not help prevent heart disease.	☐	☐
5. The American Cancer Society recommends that people eat 3 to 5 servings of fruits and vegetables daily.	☐	☐

B Study the food labels and answer the questions below.

REDUCED FAT MILK
2% Milkfat

Nutrition Facts
Serving Size 1 cup (236ml)
Servings Per Container 1

Amount Per Serving
Calories 120   Calories from Fat 45

% Daily Value*

Total Fat 5g	**8%**
Saturated Fat 3g	**15%**
Trans Fat 0g	
Cholesterol 20mg	**7%**
Sodium 120mg	**5%**
Total Carbohydrate 11g	**4%**
Dietary Fiber 0g	**0%**
Sugars 11g	
Protein 9g	**17%**

Vitamin A 10%   •   Vitamin C 4%
Calcium 30% • Iron 0% • Vitamin D 25%

*Percent Daily Values are based on a 2,000 calorie diet. Your daily values may be higher or lower depending on your calorie needs.

CHOCOLATE NONFAT MILK

Nutrition Facts
Serving Size 1 cup (236ml)
Servings Per Container 1

Amount Per Serving
Calories 80   Calories from Fat 0

% Daily Value*

Total Fat 0g	**0%**
Saturated Fat 0g	**0%**
Trans Fat 0g	
Cholesterol Less than 5mg	**0%**
Sodium 120mg	**5%**
Total Carbohydrate 11g	**4%**
Dietary Fiber 0g	**0%**
Sugars 11g	
Protein 9g	**17%**

Vitamin A 10%   •   Vitamin C 4%
Calcium 30% • Iron 0% • Vitamin D 25%

*Percent Daily Values are based on a 2,000 calorie diet. Your daily values may be higher or lower depending on your calorie needs.

1. How many servings are there in a container of reduced fat milk? _____

2. Which type of milk has more calories per serving—reduced fat milk or chocolate nonfat milk?

_____

3. Which has more fat per serving—reduced fat milk or chocolate nonfat milk? _____

4. Which has more cholesterol—reduced fat milk or chocolate nonfat milk? _____

5. How many glasses of nonfat milk would you need to drink daily to get the recommended amount of Vitamin D? _____

5 LESSON

It hurts when I breathe.

A Unscramble the questions. (There may be more than 1 correct way to write the questions.) Then answer them.

1. you eat / how / after / a big meal / do you feel

   Question: _____

   _____?

   Answer: _____

   _____

2. you do / what should / you have / a fever / when

   Question: _____?

   Answer: _____

   _____

3. fall asleep / do you / as soon as / to bed / you go / usually

   Question: _____?

   Answer: _____

4. they arrive / open your bills / do you / as soon as / in the mail

   Question: _____?

   Answer: _____

5. how hungry / you get up / are you / when / in the morning

   Question: _____?

   Answer: _____

6. did you do / what / you ate breakfast / yesterday / after

   Question: _____?

   Answer: _____

7. whenever / can you / get up / you want to

   Question: _____?

   Answer: _____

8. of food / what kind / do you prefer / you eat out / when

   Question: _____?

   Answer: _____

B Summarize the information in each conversation below.

1. A: Why did you cancel your doctor's appointment?

   B: Because I had to work that day.

   She canceled her _doctor's appointment because she had to work that day._

2. A: Why did you stop drinking coffee?

   B: Because it made me feel nervous.

   He _____

3. A: Why did they call the ambulance?

   B: Because someone had a heart attack.

   They _____

4. A: Why did you go to a physical therapist?

   B: Because I hurt my shoulder.

   She _____

5. A: Why were you late to work?

   B: I got stuck in rush hour traffic.

   He _____

C Answer these questions with your own ideas.

1. Do you think it's important to eat some fruit every day? Why or why not?

   _____

2. Do you think it's necessary to take vitamins? Why or why not?

   _____

3. Do you think it's useful to read the nutrition labels on food? Why or why not?

   _____

D Complete these sentences with your own ideas.

1. He eats a lot of fast food even though _____

2. They didn't call 911 even though _____

3. Although _____, she wouldn't go to the emergency room.

4. He wants to become a dietician even though _____

51

This accident shouldn't have happened.

A Test your knowledge of workers' health and safety by taking the quiz below. Check (✓) your guesses. Then compare answers by looking on page 165.

Workers' Health and Safety Quiz

1. Workers in the United States have certain basic health and safety rights. Which of the following is NOT one of your rights at work?

   ❏ to remove uncomfortable safety equipment

   ❏ to report safety problems to OSHA (Occupational Safety & Health Administration)

   ❏ to get payment for medical care if you get hurt on the job

   ❏ to get health and safety training

   ❏ to see the record of injuries at your workplace

2. The most common workplace injuries are _____.

   ❏ chemical burns   ❏ cuts, lacerations

   ❏ fractures   ❏ sprains, strains

3. True or False? Your boss can fire you for refusing to do unsafe work.

   ❏ true   ❏ false

4. Which industry has the most workplace fatalities?

   ❏ construction   ❏ automotive

   ❏ mining   ❏ farming

5. True or False? Office workers don't have to worry about getting injured at work.

   ❏ true   ❏ false

B Read questions 1 to 5. Then read the story on page 53 and look for answers to the questions. Write your answers in complete sentences on the lines below.

1. How did James Wright get hurt?

   _____

2. How serious were his injuries?

   _____

3. How old is he now?

   _____

4. What advice does Wright have for workers?

   _____

5. Why do you think Wright didn't ask his boss for safety training?

   _____

I Don't Remember Hitting the Ground

James Wright
Ottawa, Canada

I got a job as an apprentice tinsmith[1] and was earning high school credits. Two weeks into the job, I fell fifty feet—five stories—off a ladder and now I'm paralyzed[2] from the waist down. I was eighteen when it happened.

As it stands now, I'll be in a wheelchair for the rest of my life. The fall shattered my lower spine and six years later I'm still in a lot of pain. Usually I can only get three to five hours of sleep a night.

Getting hurt like I did, there are lots of things you miss out on. I was very active. I played a lot of sports. Now what I miss most is being able to go out and live free—I find that I'm always dependent on somebody.

After all that's happened, I don't feel resentful[3]. I have a better understanding of what I lost and what I still have. I feel grateful[4] to be alive. An accident like that can happen so easily, at the snap of your fingers. So if you don't feel safe, tell your boss and ask for training. I never received any proper safety training. If I had, I might not have fallen off that ladder.

Source: From "I don't remember hitting the ground." James Wright—Ottawa from www.yworker.com. Reprinted with permission of Ontario's Workplace Safety and Insurance Board.

_____
[1] tinsmith: person who makes things from tin or other light metals
[2] paralyzed: unable to move
[3] resentful: angry or hurt
[4] grateful: thankful

★★★

TAKE IT OUTSIDE: Interview someone you know who has a job. Ask the questions below and record the person's answers. Then tell your classmates what you learned.

Questions	Answers
1) What kind of work do you do?	
2) What kinds of hazards are at your job?	
3) What kind of safety training did you get for your job?	
4) Do you wear any protective clothing?	
5) What are the most common types of injuries at your workplace?	

★★★

TAKE IT ONLINE: Use your favorite search engine to look for OSHA's website. Then list 3 new things you learned about this organization from the website.

1. _____

2. _____

3. _____

Addiction is a problem.

A Read questions 1 to 4. Then read the story below and look for answers to the questions. Write your answers on the lines.

1. What is an addiction?

_____

2. Why did the writer think she was addicted to the computer?

_____

3. What problems do you think the writer's addiction caused for her?

_____

4. What are three more things you could do to stop this type of addiction?

_____ *sell your computer* _____   _____

_____   _____

Was I Addicted to the Computer?

by Tina Chang

I think I was addicted to the computer when I was in my second year of high school. At that time, the first thing that I did after school was turn on the computer. I would spend a lot of time checking my email even though I didn't get very many email messages. I spent hours and hours in front of my computer screen and surfed the Internet for a long time. Though I knew I should stop to do my homework, I just couldn't.

This situation lasted[1] for about two months, and then I became aware that I was spending too much time online. It was not easy to break the habit, but I still tried hard to do so. Now I am no longer addicted to the computer; I spend less than one hour in front of the computer screen each day.

Source: "Was I Addicted to the Computer?" by Tina Chang, *TOPICS* Online Magazine, www.topics-mag.com. Used by permission of TOPICS Online Magazine.

_____

[1] lasted: continued

B Use the graph below to complete these sentences.

1. Alcohol is involved in _____ of the fatalities on highways.

2. More than _____ of the deaths in fires are alcohol related.

3. _____ of the accidents at work are alcohol related.

4. Alcohol was involved in _____ of the deaths of pedestrians.

How Alcohol Harms Society

Drinking too much not only harms individuals but society as a whole. Here is how alcohol abuse is related to many of our nation's most difficult problems. The numbers represent the percentage of all cases that are related to alcohol.

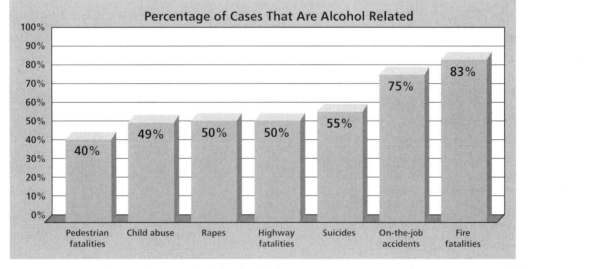

Source: "Percentage of Cases That Are Alcohol-Related", from Prevention's *Giant Book of Health Facts*, Rodale Press, 1991.

C What kinds of problems can each of these addictions cause for individuals, families, and communities? List 3 ideas for each category.

Drinking Alcohol	Gambling	Smoking	Taking Illegal Drugs
car accidents *accidents at work* *bad health*			

TAKE IT ONLINE: Use your favorite search engine to find the information below. Write down the addresses of the sites and share them with your classmates.

1. Find a site that gives information about treatments for addictions.

2. Find a site that gives information about drug abuse signs and symptoms.

3. Find a site that gives information about alcohol addiction.

REVIEW LESSON

Practice Test

DIRECTIONS: Read the food label to answer the next 6 questions. Use the Answer Sheet.

INGREDIENTS: ROASTED PEANUTS, CORN SYRUP SOLIDS, SUGAR, SOY PROTEIN, SALT, VEGETABLE OIL.

Nutrition Facts

Serving Size 2 Tbsp

Servings Per Container about 14

Amount Per Serving

Calories 190	Calories from Fat 100

	% Daily Value
Total Fat 12g	19%
Saturated Fat 2.5g	12%
Cholesterol 0mg	0%
Sodium 190 mg	8%
Total Carbohydrate 15g	5%
Protein 7g	

ANSWER SHEET

1. (A) (B) (C) (D)
2. (A) (B) (C) (D)
3. (A) (B) (C) (D)
4. (A) (B) (C) (D)
5. (A) (B) (C) (D)
6. (A) (B) (C) (D)
7. (A) (B) (C) (D)
8. (A) (B) (C) (D)
9. (A) (B) (C) (D)
10. (A) (B) (C) (D)

1. Which of these is <u>not</u> an ingredient in this peanut butter?
   A. peanuts   C. salt
   B. butter   D. sugar

2. How large is one serving of peanut butter?
   A. 2 teaspoons   C. 2 cups
   B. 2 tablespoons   D. 2 pints

3. How many grams of fat are there in a serving of this peanut butter?
   A. 2.5   C. 12
   B. 23   D. 0

4. About how many servings are there in this jar of peanut butter?
   A. 2   C. 100
   B. 14   D. 190

5. If you ate this whole jar of peanut butter, about how many calories would you consume?
   A. 190   C. 2660
   B. 380   D. 5320

6. This peanut butter does <u>not</u> contain any _____.
   A. salt   C. carbohydrates
   B. sugar   D. cholesterol

DIRECTIONS: Read the information below to answer the next 4 questions. Use the Answer Sheet on page 56.

> Doctors are sometimes said to fall into two main groups: primary care physicians (sometimes referred to as generalists) and specialists. The term *primary care* refers to the medical fields that treat most common health problems—family medicine, pediatrics, and in some cases obstetrics and gynecology.
>
> Specialists concentrate on particular types of illnesses or problems that affect specific tissues or organ systems in the body. They may treat patients with complicated illnesses who are referred to them by primary care physicians or by other specialists.
>
> Whatever their focus, all physicians must hold one of two degrees. Most have an M.S. (doctor of medicine) degree, and some hold a D.O. (doctor of osteopathy) degree. The two types of degrees reflect different theories and practices of medicine, but medical licensing authorities recognize both types of doctors.
>
> Doctors may hold many other degrees as well as medical degrees. Some have Ph.D. (doctor of philosophy) or master's degrees in the sciences or in fields like public health, hospital administration, or education.
>
> Source: http://www.vh.org/

7. What is the topic of this article?

   A. medical specialties
   B. theories of medicine
   C. types of doctors
   D. primary care physicians

8. Which statement is true about all specialists?

   A. They have PhDs.
   B. They hold a D.O. degree.
   C. They refer patients to primary care physicians.
   D. They have extra training in one area.

9. According to the article, which of these is a specialist?

   A. a primary care physician
   B. a cardiologist
   C. a pediatrician
   D. a generalist

10. In the second paragraph, the word "complicated" means _____.

   A. difficult
   B. simple
   C. common
   D. new

HOW DID YOU DO? Count the number of correct answers on your answer sheet. Record this number in the bar graph on the inside back cover.

Spotlight: Reading

A Read the definitions and the sentences below. Use context clues to choose the correct definition for the word in each sentence. Circle the number of the definition.

fatigue *noun*

1 extreme tiredness

2 *plural* military clothes

3 the weakening of a material due to stress

1. Poor eating habits can cause **fatigue**.   1 2 3
2. **Fatigue** is a common symptom of many illnesses.   1 2 3
3. The building collapsed because of metal **fatigue**.   1 2 3
4. What color are his **fatigues**?   1 2 3

bill *noun*

1 a written statement of the amount of money to be paid

2 a piece of paper money

3 a written proposal for a new law

5. Have you paid your **bills** yet?   1 2 3
6. Do you know how your senator voted on the health care **bill**?   1 2 3
7. Do you have a ten dollar **bill** on you?   1 2 3
8. How much was the hospital's **bill**?   1 2 3

perform *verb*

1 to carry out an action

2 to present or act in a performance such as a play, concert, or dance.

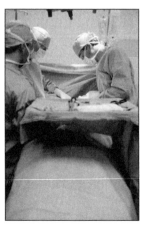

9. Have you ever **performed** in a play?   1 2
10. They **performed** bravely in the emergency.   1 2
11. The doctor **performed** the surgery in just an hour.   1 2

B Read the information and use context clues to guess the meaning of the boldfaced words. Then match each word to a synonym in the chart below. Write the words on the lines.

Q: How important are nutrition and dietary factors in health and chronic disease prevention?

A: The Surgeon General's Report on Nutrition and Health in 1988 noted that 2/3 of all deaths are due to diseases **associated** with diet. The report also says that the three most important personal habits that **influence** health are smoking, alcohol consumption, and diet. For the two out of three adults who do not drink alcohol **excessively** or smoke, the single most important personal choice influencing long-term health is what they eat.

In 1997, a report by the World Cancer Research Fund and the American Institute for Cancer Research stated that recommended diets **in conjunction** with physical activity and normal BMI (body mass index) could reduce cancer **incidence** by 30–40%.

For heart disease, the report by the 1989 National Academy of Sciences **projected** that 20% of deaths could be avoided by reducing fats and increasing fruits, vegetables, breads, cereals, and legumes (dry beans and peas).

Source: http://www.cdc.gov/

Words from the article

1. associated _____connected_____
2. influence _____
3. excessively _____
4. in conjunction _____
5. incidence _____
6. projected _____

Synonyms

a. together
b. suddenly
c. necessary
d. connected
e. affect
f. frequency
g. a lot
h. encourage
i. predicted

C Use the article in Activity B to answer these questions.

1. What 3 things have the biggest negative effect on people's health?

_____

2. In addition to eating healthy food, what does the article say you can do to reduce your risk of cancer?

_____

Spotlight: Writing

A Eight punctuation marks are missing from the article below. Write the correct punctuation mark in each circle.

Taking Care of Your Health

People in the U.S. pay for their own medical care. Medical care is expensive ◯ so many people buy health insurance. You should get health insurance for yourself and your family as soon as possible.

Employers may offer health insurance as a benefit to their employees. Some employers pay all of your monthly health insurance fee ◯ and some pay only part of the fee. This monthly fee is called a "premium." You may need to pay part of the premium ◯ Usually ◯ employers will deduct the employee's part of the premium from their paycheck.

Doctors send their bills to your health insurance company. The health insurance company will pay for some or all of your medical bills. This is sometimes called a "co-payment. ◯

If you do not have health insurance ◯ you may be able to get federal or state health care assistance. In general ◯ most states provide some type of assistance to children and pregnant women. Check with the public health department of your state or town.

If you need urgent medical care ◯ you can go to the emergency room of the nearest hospital. Most hospitals are required by federal law to treat patients with a medical emergency even if the person cannot pay.

Source: http://uscis.gov/

B Read the article in Activity A and answer the questions below.

1. Why is it important to buy health insurance in the United States?

   _____

   _____

2. What is a "co-payment"?

   _____

   _____

3. If you don't have medical insurance, what should you do if you have a medical emergency?

   _____

   _____

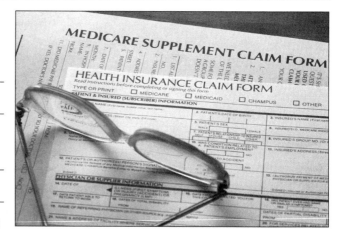

C Add the missing punctuation to the personal letters below.

September 12 2005

Dear Tricia

My apologies for not
returning your book sooner I
enjoyed it a lot and I thank
you for recommending it to me

Sincerely

Chandra

October 15 2006

Dear Phil and Ben

Please forgive me for not
writing sooner to thank you for
the beautiful flowers you sent
when I was in the hospital It
was very thoughtful of you to
think of me and having the
flowers cheered me up

My best
Oscar

D Write a letter to someone you know. Remember to punctuate your letter correctly.

LESSON 1

They marched on Washington.

A Study the map of Washington D.C. and read the sentences below. Check (✓) *True* or *False*.

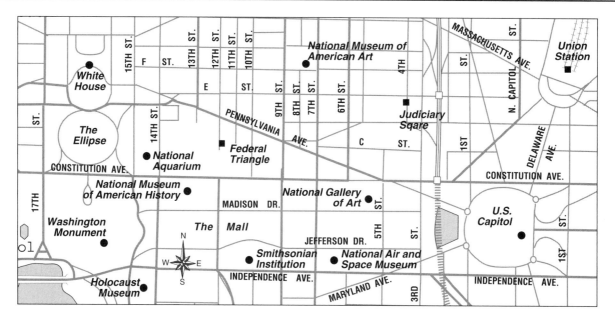

	True	False
1. The Mall is between the Washington Monument and the U.S. Capitol.	☐	☐
2. The White House is directly south of the Washington Monument.	☐	☐
3. To get from the White House to the Capitol building, you can go west on Pennsylvania Avenue.	☐	☐
4. Jefferson Drive runs parallel to Independence Avenue.	☐	☐
5. The National Museum of American History is across the Mall from the Smithsonian Institution.	☐	☐
6. To get from the Capitol building to the Washington Monument, you have to cross 7th St.	☐	☐
7. To get from the Washington Monument to the White House, you have to cross Independence Avenue.	☐	☐
8. To get from the National Air and Space Museum to the National Museum of American History, you can go east on Jefferson Drive and then north on 14th Street.	☐	☐

B Correct the false sentences in Activity A.

_____

_____

_____

_____

_____

C Unscramble the questions. Then match each question to an answer below. Write the letter of the answer on the line.

1. the colors / are / the U.S. / what / flag / of

   _____? _____

2. stars / how many / on / are / the U.S. flag

   _____? _____

3. color / on the U.S. flag / the stars / what / are

   _____? _____

4. what / represent / do / on the flag / the stars

   _____? _____

5. stripes / on the flag / are / how many

   _____? _____

6. do / what / on the flag / the stripes / represent

   _____? _____

7. is / the United States / what / Capitol

   _____? _____

8. the capital / is / what / of / the United States

   _____? _____

Answers

a. the fifty states	c. Washington, D.C.	e. fifty	g. the place where Congress meets
b. thirteen	d. red, white, and blue	f. the original 13 colonies	h. white

D Compare the 2 U.S. flags and write 6 ideas in the Venn Diagram below.

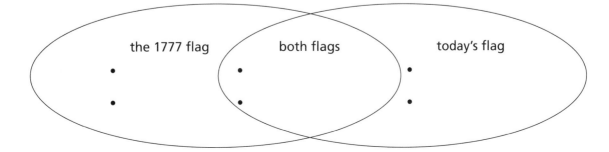

the 1777 flag   both flags   today's flag

2 **LESSON**

It's your right.

A Complete the questions below with the correct form of the word in the box. Then answer the questions.

NOUN	VERB	ADJECTIVE
1. authority	authorize	XXXXX
2. treatment	treat	XXXXX
3. honesty	XXXXX	honest
4. gathering	gather	XXXXX
5. religion	XXXXX	religious
6. belief	believe	believable
7. tolerance	tolerate	tolerant
8. registration	register	XXXXX
9. election	elect	XXXXX
10. respect	respect	respectful

1. In the United States, who has the _____ to make new laws?

   _____

2. What is an example of unfair _____ of an employee by an employer?

   _____

3. How can you tell when someone isn't being _____?

   _____

4. Where in your city do large groups of people sometimes _____?

   _____

5. What is the closest _____ building to your school?

   _____

6. Do you _____ everything you read in the newspaper?

   _____

7. What kind of behavior is difficult to _____?

   _____

8. Can you_____to vote by mail?

   _____

9. When is the next presidential _____?

_____

10. How can young people show_____to older people?

_____

B Read this information and answer the questions below.

The Bill of Rights

The first ten amendments, or changes, to the U.S. Constitution protect certain freedoms and rights of U.S. citizens by limiting the power of the government. These ten amendments are called The Bill of Rights.

First Amendment Guarantees the rights of freedom of speech, religion, press, peaceable assembly, and to petition the government.

Second Amendment Guarantees the right to bear arms.

Third Amendment Says the government cannot force citizens to house soldiers in their homes during peacetime and without permission.

Fourth Amendment States that the government cannot search or take a person's property without a warrant.

Fifth Amendment Says that a person cannot be tried twice for the same crime or forced to testify against himself or herself.

Sixth Amendment States that people have the right to a fair trial with adequate legal representation.

Seventh Amendment Guarantees a trial by jury in most cases.

Eighth Amendment Prohibits all "cruel and unusual punishment."

Ninth Amendment Says that people have other rights in addition to those listed in the Constitution.

Tenth Amendment States that the powers that the Constitution does not give to the national government belong to the states and to the citizens.

---

1. Which amendment says you have other rights, in addition to those listed in the Constitution? _____

2. Which amendment allows you to disagree with an action of the government? _____

3. Which amendment prevents the government from telling newspapers what to print? _____

4. Which amendment prevents the government from forcing people to go church? _____

5. Which amendment says the government cannot enter your house without a strong reason? _____

6. Which amendment prevents the government from stopping a protest march? _____

LESSON 3

Should high school be compulsory?

A Read these opinions and tell if you agree or disagree. Check (✓) your ideas.

1. In my opinion, all citizens should be required to vote in the presidential election.

   ❏ I think so too.   ❏ I'm not sure about that.

2. I wish they would raise the speed limit on highways.

   ❏ So do I.   ❏ You do?

3. I think health care should be free.

   ❏ Me too.   ❏ Really? Why is that?

4. I don't like to pay taxes.

   ❏ Neither do I.   ❏ Really? Why not?

5. I don't think children should have to go to school until they are 16.

   ❏ I don't either.   ❏ Really? Why is that?

6. I enjoy reading about history.

   ❏ I do too.   ❏ You do?

B Complete the conversations so that the people agree.

1. A: I think we should vote in the election tomorrow.

   B: _____

2. A: I don't think people should keep guns at home.

   B: _____

3. A: I think it's important to get a college education.

   B: _____

4. A: I think the voting age should be changed.

   B: _____

5. A: I don't think schools should sell junk food to children.

   B: _____

6. A: I think it's important to study history.

   B: _____

7. A: I prefer coeducational schools.

   B: _____

8. A: I think our public transportation system should be a lot better.

   B: _____

C Complete the sentences with words from the box.

tolerate	discriminatory	peaceful	encourage
compulsory	protest	participate	coeducational
honestly	responsibility	policy	requirements

1. In some countries voting is _____; you have to do it.

2. The demonstration on the Washington Mall was _____; no one caused any problems.

3. Allowing men to vote but not women is _____.

4. It is the _____ of every citizen to vote in elections.

5. It's important for citizens to _____ in the government. They can do things such as writing letters to their representatives and voting in elections.

6. I can't _____ very hot weather; it makes me feel sick.

7. It is the _____ of the government to encourage people to vote but not to require them to vote.

8. If you don't want your children to attend a _____ school, you will have to send them to a private school.

9. I _____ don't know who is responsible for making this mess, but I hope I find out.

10. The _____ for entrance into a university vary from one school to another.

11. I think it's important for parents to _____ their children to study hard in school.

12. She didn't _____ when the man demanded her purse. She gave it to him and said nothing.

D Complete the sentences with information about yourself. Choose the correct word in each pair of antonyms.

1. I am _____ about the cost of education. (concerned / unconcerned)

2. I think I am _____ of people with different lifestyles from mine. (tolerant / intolerant)

3. I think it's _____ to vote in elections. (important / unimportant)

4. I believe that it is _____ to write letters to your representatives in Washington. (useful / useless)

5. It's _____ to leave very young children at home alone. (responsible / irresponsible)

6. I am _____ about politics in my state. (informed / uninformed)

7. I am _____ about where I will be living at this time next year. (sure / unsure)

9. I prefer to do _____ activities in my free time. (active / passive)

10. I think it should be _____ to talk on a cell phone while driving a car. (legal / illegal)

67

LESSON 4

Government Agencies

A Complete the questions with words from the box. Then answer the questions.

disasters	investigates	consumer
recall	obey	discrimination
acronym	enforces	

1. What does the _____ FEMA stand for?

   _____

2. Why might an automobile company _____ one of its cars?

   _____

3. Which U.S. government agency works to stop _____ at work?

   _____

4. What kinds of _____ does the Federal Emergency Management Agency help communities recover from?

   _____

5. What is the acronym for the _____ Product Safety Commission?

   _____

6. Which U.S. government agency _____ clean air laws?

   _____

7. Which U.S. agency _____ federal crimes?

   _____

8. Who makes sure that businesses _____ the law?

   _____

B Describe a problem or an emergency you or someone you know experienced. Answer the questions below in your writing.

- What was the problem or emergency?
- What happened?
- What help or assistance was available?
- What could have been done to avoid the problem or emergency?

_____

_____

_____

_____

_____

C Read the information from a website. Use it to answer the questions below.

⊠ ⊟ ⊞   **www.osha.gov**

U.S. Department of Labor
Occupational Safety & Health Administration
www.osha.gov

Search [＿＿＿＿＿＿＿＿] GO

Site Index: A B C D E F G H I J K L M N O P Q R S T U V W X Y Z

Making a Positive Difference

OSHA Saves Lives

1 "Get out of that trench," OSHA Inspector Robert Dickinson ordered a worker in an unsafe trench by the side of the road near El Paso, Texas. El Paso Assistant Area Director Mario Solano had noticed the trench earlier, and he sent Dickinson and Elia Casillas to check it out. Thirty seconds after the employee got out of the trench, the wall near where he had been standing collapsed. Warning the worker to leave the trench prevented the worker from experiencing a serious injury.

2 On June 10, OSHA compliance officers from the El Paso District Office helped prevent a terrible accident. The two officers were sent to the site of a tower under construction. At the construction site, the two officers found that workers on the tower did not have proper equipment to protect them from an 80 foot fall. The OSHA officers talked with the employer who then instructed the workers to get off the tower. The employer agreed to install a safety system to protect the workers from a fall.

3 In August, two workers were washing windows from a scaffold high up above the ground. Suddenly the scaffold broke, and the two men remained hanging in the air. Luckily the two workers were using the proper safety equipment and they didn't fall to the ground. Soon, the fire department was able to rescue them.

Source: http://www.osha.gov/

---

1. The information above is from the website of which government agency?

2. In the first story, why did the inspector tell the employee to get out of the trench?

3. In the second story, what was the problem with the tower?

4. In the second story, what did the employer need to do?

5. In the third story, why didn't the workers get hurt?

6. What do these three stories have in common?

7. How is the third story different from the first two?

LESSON 5

He was elected in 1789.

A Add the missing verb forms to the chart. Then complete the sentences below with the passive form of the verbs.

SIMPLE FORM	PAST FORM	PAST PARTICIPLE
1. write	*wrote*	*written*
2. call		
3. sign		
4. celebrate		
5. elect		
6. build		
7. give		
8. allow		

1. Do you know when the U.S. Constitution _____?

2. Can you tell me what the first ten amendments to the Constitution _____?

3. Do you know when the U.S. Declaration of Independence _____?

4. Do you know when Independence Day _____ in the U.S.?

5. Can you tell me when the first U.S. president _____?

6. Do you know when the White House _____?

7. Do you remember when women in the U.S. _____ the right to vote for the first time?

8. Do you know when 18-year-olds _____ to vote?

B Change the sentences from active to passive.

1. Adela wrote this letter.

   _____

2. Someone from Florida bought my house.

   _____

3. My brother took this photograph.

   _____

4. My mother made this sweater.

   _____

5. I paid my taxes on time.

   _____

6. His landlord treated him unfairly.

_____

7. Marilyn sang the song.

_____

8. A truck hit my car.

_____

9. Someone from the newspaper interviewed me.

_____

10. The police closed the road.

_____

C Add the missing verbs to the paragraphs below. Choose the active or passive form of the verbs in the list below.

(1) protects / is protected
(2) makes up / is made up
(3) guarantees / is guaranteed
(4) can punish / can be punished
(5) made up / was made up
(6) ruled / were ruled
(7) should govern / should be governed
(8) issued / were issued
(9) said / was said
(10) wrote / was written
(11) elected / was elected

The government of the United States _____ (1) the rights of every person. The United States _____ (2) of people from many different backgrounds and beliefs, but each person _____ (3) the same rights. No one _____ (4) for having a belief or opinion that is different.

Before the United States became an independent country, it _____ (5) of 13 colonies that _____ (6) by Great Britain. In 1776, the people in the colonies decided they _____ (7) themselves. Representatives from the colonies _____ (8) a Declaration of Independence. This document _____ (9) that the colonies were now free and independent. Thomas Jefferson _____ (10) the Declaration of Independence. Later, he _____ (11) the third president of the United States.

71

What are a tenant's rights?

A Whose responsibility is it? Check (✓) *Landlord* or *Tenant*.

Whose responsibility is it to _____?	the landlord	the tenant
1. provide locks and keys for doors	☐	☐
2. get rid of insects, rodents, etc.	☐	☐
3. put trash in trash cans	☐	☐
4. repair the heating system if it breaks	☐	☐
5. provide smoke detectors	☐	☐
6. keep the rental property clean so it doesn't attract insects, rodents, etc.	☐	☐
7. replace batteries in smoke detectors	☐	☐

B Read each person's problem below. Then use the information on page 73 to answer each person's question.

---

1. I live in a large apartment building and I often see the landlord go into people's apartments when they are not at home. My neighbor even came home one day when the landlord was in the apartment. He told her he was checking the smoke detectors. Does he really have the right to enter our apartments whenever he wants to? What can we do?
   —Stella

   Problem:
   Possible response:

2. The shower in my apartment doesn't work properly. I told my landlord about it three weeks ago, but he still hasn't fixed it. I have left him several messages on his answering machine but he hasn't returned my calls. What should I do?
   —Hamid

   Problem:
   Possible response:

3. During the summer my landlord sometimes turns the electricity off. He says he is only doing this to make repairs but I know this isn't true. What can I do?
   —Z.B.

   Problem:
   Possible response:

4. There's something wrong with the refrigerator in our apartment. We told the landlord about it and he promised to either fix it or buy us a new one. That was two months ago and still nothing has happened. What can we do?
   —Taka

   Problem:
   Possible response:

IllinoisLawHelp.org

IllinoisLawHelp.org
Providing Legal Information for Illinois Residents

Search

Choose a topic:

Consumer Law   Going to Court   Public Benefits
Criminal Law   Health Care   Senior Citizens
Disability   **Housing**   Taxes
Education   Immigration   Work
Family Law   Life Planning

Tenant's Rights Fact Sheet

What must a landlord do?
The landlord must:
- keep the home up to local building code;
- keep the home so you can safely live in it;
- give you written notice before ending the lease; and
- not enter the home without telling you in advance, unless it is an emergency.

What must a tenant do?
- keep the home clean;
- not change the home unless the landlord says it is okay;
- pay the rent when it is due;
- obey the lease; and
- tell the landlord about any problems with the home.

How do I get the landlord to make repairs?
You must tell the landlord about the problem. If the landlord does not fix the problem, write the landlord a letter. Send the letter by certified mail. Ask for a return receipt. Keep a copy of the letter.

You may complain to the building department about problems. If the problems are serious, they may condemn the home. Then you would have to move.

If the landlord promises to make repairs, send the landlord a letter saying what the landlord promised to do.

What if the landlord turns the water off?
Water, gas, and electricity are utilities. The landlord may only turn the utilities off to make repairs. The landlord may not turn the utilities off for any other reason. If the landlord does, you can sue the landlord.

TAKE IT ONLINE: Use your favorite search engine to look for the rights of tenants in a state other than Illinois. Make a Venn Diagram like the one below. Show the similarities and differences in tenant rights in Illinois and the state you chose.

Illinois   both states   _____

Voting Rights

A Read questions 1 to 5 below. Then read the FAQs and look for answers to the questions.

1. How old do you have to be to vote in the United States? _____

2. If you move to another town in the same state, do you have to register to vote again? YES NO

3. If November 1st is a Tuesday, what is the date of the presidential election? _____

4. Can I choose where I want to vote? YES NO

5. Which of these people can vote? Check (✓) CAN VOTE or CAN'T VOTE.

1. Mayela
   • is 70 years old
   • is a U.S. citizen
   • moved to Florida last year
   • hasn't registered to vote in Florida
   ☐ CAN VOTE   ☐ CAN'T VOTE

2. Fernando
   • his 18th birthday is on 11/1
   • has registered to vote
   • is a U.S. citizen
   • does not have a job
   ☐ CAN VOTE   ☐ CAN'T VOTE

3. Lilian
   • is 28 years old
   • just became a U.S. citizen
   • has registered to vote
   • can't speak English
   ☐ CAN VOTE   ☐ CAN'T VOTE

FREQUENTLY ASKED QUESTIONS ABOUT VOTING

1) Who can vote in the United States?
In order to vote, you must a) be at least 18 years old by Election Day, b) be a United States citizen, and c) be registered to vote.

2) How do you register to vote?
To *register* means to "sign up." When you register, your name is added to a list of voters. If you move to a new town or city, you must register again to vote. Registration deadlines vary from state to state. In some states, you have to register 30 days before the election. In most places you can register by mail or online.

3) When do you vote?
The election for President is on the Tuesday after the first Monday in November. Other elections are held at different times.

4) Where do you vote?
Your voter registration card tells you where to vote. Most people vote in a place in their neighborhood.

B Answer these questions about the application form below. Circle your answers.

1. In which section should you write the date?	1	4	9
2. In which section should you sign your name?	1	3	9
3. If your home address is the same as your mailing address, which section should you leave blank?	2	3	5
4. Which of these sections can you leave blank?	1	5	9
5. Which section asks you to look at the special instructions for your state?	3	4	7

Voter Registration Application
Before completing this form, review the General, Application, and State specific instructions.

Are you a citizen of the United States of America? ☐ Yes ☐ No

Will you be 18 years old on or before election day? ☐ Yes ☐ No

This space for office use only.

If you checked "No" in response to either of these questions, do not complete form.
(Please see state-specific instructions for rules regarding eligibility to register prior to age 18.)

1 (Circle one) Mr. Mrs. Miss Ms. | Last Name | First Name | Middle Name(s) | (Circle one) Jr Sr II III IV

2 Home address | Apt. or Lot # | City/Town | State | Zip Code

3 Address Where You Get Your Mail if Different From Above | City/Town | State | Zip Code

4 Date of Birth ___ / ___ / ___ (Month Day Year)

5 Telephone Number (optional)

6 ID Number - (See Item 6 in the instructions for your State)

7 Choice of Party (see item 7 in the instructions for your State)

8 Race or Ethnic Group (see item 8 in the instructions for your State)

9 I have reviewed my state's instructions and I swear/affirm that:
- I am a United States citizen.
- I meet the eligibility requirements of my state and subscribe to any oath required.
- The information I have provided is true to the best of my knowledge under penalty of perjury. If I have provided false information, I may be fined, imprisoned, or (if not a U.S. citizen) deported from or refused entry to the United States.

Please sign full name (or put mark) ▲

Date: ___ / ___ / ___ (Month Day Year)

If you are registering to vote for the first time: please refer to the application instructions for information on submitting copies of valid identification documents with this form.

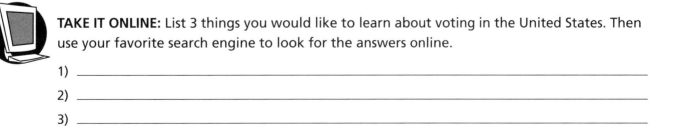

TAKE IT ONLINE: List 3 things you would like to learn about voting in the United States. Then use your favorite search engine to look for the answers online.

1) _____

2) _____

3) _____

Practice Test

A Use the information below to answer the next 5 questions. Use the Answer Sheet.

KNOW YOUR RIGHTS: FEDERAL LAWS PROTECT EMPLOYEES

Several federal laws forbid employers from discriminating against people looking for a job. The United States has laws forbidding discrimination because of:

- Race, color, religion, country of origin, and sex (Civil Rights Act)
- Age (Age Discrimination in Employment Act)
- Disabilities (Americans with Disabilities Act)
- Sex (Equal Pay Act)

For more information about these protections, visit the U.S. Equal Employment Opportunity Commission website at http://www.eeoc.gov or call 1-800-669-4000 or 1-800-669-6820 (for hearing impaired).

Other laws help keep work places safe, provide for leave in cases of family or medical emergencies, and provide temporary funds for unemployed workers. Visit the U.S. Department of Labor website at http://www.dol.gov for more information about workers' rights.

ANSWER SHEET

1	Ⓐ	Ⓑ	Ⓒ	Ⓓ
2	Ⓐ	Ⓑ	Ⓒ	Ⓓ
3	Ⓐ	Ⓑ	Ⓒ	Ⓓ
4	Ⓐ	Ⓑ	Ⓒ	Ⓓ
5	Ⓐ	Ⓑ	Ⓒ	Ⓓ
6	Ⓐ	Ⓑ	Ⓒ	Ⓓ
7	Ⓐ	Ⓑ	Ⓒ	Ⓓ
8	Ⓐ	Ⓑ	Ⓒ	Ⓓ
9	Ⓐ	Ⓑ	Ⓒ	Ⓓ
10	Ⓐ	Ⓑ	Ⓒ	Ⓓ

1. Which act protects someone in a wheelchair from discrimination on the job?

   A. Equal Pay Act
   B. Americans with Disabilities Act
   C. Age Discrimination in Employment Act
   D. Civil Rights Act

2. Which act protects you from discrimination because of your religion?

   A. Equal Pay Act
   B. Americans with Disabilities Act
   C. Age Discrimination in Employment Act
   D. Civil Rights Act

3. If you want more information about safety at work, what can you do?

   A. Call 1-800-669-4000.
   B. Call 911.
   C. Visit www.eeoc.gov.
   D. Visit www.dol.gov.

4. Choose the best dictionary meaning for the word "leave" in the article.

   A. go away permanently
   B. to have as a result
   C. a period away from work
   D. permission

5. What does the word "fund" mean in this article?

   A. a large amount of something
   B. money for a specific purpose
   C. a savings account
   D. to sponsor

B Use the information in the graph to answer the next 5 questions. Use the Answer Sheet on page 76.

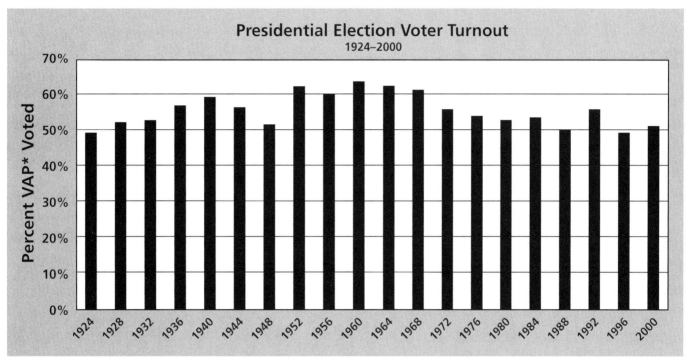

Presidential Election Voter Turnout
1924–2000

*VAP: Voting Age Population

6. In which year was voter turnout the highest?

A. 1932

B. 1940

C. 1960

D. 1980

7. In which year below was voter turnout the lowest?

A. 1928

B. 1948

C. 1996

D. 2000

8. Which statement is true?

A. In 1956, 60% of the people didn't vote.

B. The number of people who have voted has decreased steadily.

C. More people voted in 1940 than in 1924.

D. More people vote now than in the past.

9. What information is provided in the graph?

A. The percent of women who voted.

B. The percent of people who didn't vote.

C. The percent of people who voted.

D. The number of people who voted in each election.

10. In which two years was the voter turnout about the same?

A. 1948 and 2000

B. 1924 and 1960

C. 1988 and 1992

D. 1928 and 1964

HOW DID YOU DO? Count the number of correct answers on your answer sheet. Record this number in the bar graph on the inside back cover.

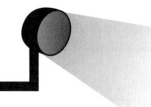

Spotlight: Reading

A Skim the article on page 79 and then complete the sentences below.

1. The title is _____.

2. The headings are _____ and _____.

3. This reading is about _____.

B Scan the article on page 79 to find the information below.

1. The names of the two parts of the U.S. Congress: _____ _____

2. The number of people in each part of the U.S. Congress: _____ _____

C Read the article and take notes in the chart below.

	The U.S. House of Representatives	The U.S. Senate
1. Total number		
2. Number per state		
3. Length of term		
4. Responsibilities		

D Think of 3 more things you would like to learn about the U.S. Congress. Write your questions below. Talk about your questions with your classmates.

- _____
- _____
- _____

TAKE IT ONLINE: Visit the websites of the U.S. Congress to find out about current activities in the House and Senate. The House of Representatives' website is http://www.house.gov/. The Senate's website is http://www.senate.gov/. Share what you learned with your classmates.

All About the U.S. Congress

Citizens of the United States vote in free elections to choose people to represent them in the U.S. Congress. Congress has the responsibility of making the laws for our nation. Congress is made up of the House of Representatives and the Senate.

The U.S. House of Representatives

People in each state vote to choose members of the House of Representatives. There are 435 members of the House of Representatives, which is often called "the House." The number of representatives from each state depends on how many people live in that state. States are divided into districts. People living in each district vote for someone to represent their district in the House. Each representative serves for two years, and then people have another chance to vote for them or for a different person to represent them. Representatives can serve in Congress for an unlimited period of time.

The House of Representatives makes laws, but it also has some special responsibilities. Only the House of Representatives can:

- Make laws about taxes.

- Decide if a government official accused of committing a crime against the country should be put on trial in the Senate. This is called "impeachment."

The U.S. Senate

There are 100 Senators in the U.S. Senate. People in each state vote to choose two Senators to represent them in Congress. Senators serve for six years, and then people have another chance to vote for them or for a different person to represent them. Senators can serve in Congress for an unlimited period of time. Senators make laws, but they also have special responsibilities. Only the Senate can:

- Say "yes" or "no" to any agreements the President makes with other countries or organizations of countries. These are called "treaties."

- Say "yes" or "no" to any person the President chooses for high-level jobs, such as Supreme Court judges or officials to run the federal departments, such as the Department of Education or the Department of Health and Human Services.

- Hold a trial for a government official who commits a crime against the United States.

Source: http://uscis.gov/

Spotlight: Writing

A Read each sentence and identify the writer's purpose. Choose from the ideas in the box.

Purposes for Writing

- to give an opinion
- to ask for information
- to ask for help
- to give information
- to persuade
- to invite
- to thank

1. Would you like to come to dinner tonight? _____ *to invite* _____

2. Can you take this to the post office for me? _____

3. Did you know the schools will be closed tomorrow? _____

4. Do you know the name of a good restaurant? _____

5. I think we need a better public transportation system. _____

6. Please come to the party. A lot of people you know will be there. _____

7. It was very nice of you to help my father get to the store. _____

8. Is there any chance you could take me to school tomorrow? _____

B Read the letter and identify the writer's purpose.

The writer's purpose for writing this letter was to _____

_____

3566 Seventh Street
Boston, MA 02101
October 10, 2005

Merit Health Insurance Co.
5997 Langdon Road
Baltimore, Maryland 21201

Dear Sir/Madam:

This letter is to hereby notify you of my intent to cancel my health policy with Merit Health Insurance, effective November 1, 2005.

Sincerely,

Sarah Miles

Sarah Miles

C Read the letter and answer the questions below.

5449 Orion Road
Pittsfield, Idaho 83501
June 16, 2005

Office of Senator Jones
United States Senate
Washington, D.C. 20510

Dear Senator Jones:

I am writing this letter to voice my support for the ban on ATVs in our parks. I feel strongly that the presence of these vehicles is harmful to the wildlife, water resources, and passive recreation opportunities in our parks. ATV users may deserve a place to use their vehicles, but it should not be in an area where people walk and animals live.

I urge you to support this ban.

Sincerely,

Jacob Marden

Jacob Marden

1. Who is the sender of this letter? _____

2. What salutation did the writer use? _____

3. What is the writer's purpose for writing? _____

4. What does the writer give an opinion about? _____

5. What closing does the writer use? _____

6. Do you think this is an effective letter? Why or why not?

_____

_____

LESSON 1

Everything must go.

A Read the advertisements and answer the questions below.

Ad #1

Bob's Furniture
Family Owned and Operated

Bring this ad to get a **10%** discount on your first purchase.

Ad #2

MARDEN'S

Summer Special
SALE

All sweaters
10% Off

Ad #3

Jimmy's Diner

Breakfast Special*
JUST $1.00
5 Eggs Any Style
Plus Coffee

5495 Ridgely Road

*Served between 3 A.M. and 5 A.M. only.

Ad #4

RENT A WRECK
CAR RENTALS

$15.00 A DAY + .05 PER MILE

You won't find anything cheaper!

Call 555-3499

Ad #5

DOOGAN'S
SALE 50% Off

AYERS
HAIRBRUSHES

Buy two and get the second one
for **50% OFF**

$9.99 Original Price
$4.99 Sale Price

1. If you want to get 10% off a piece of furniture at Bob's, what do you have to do?

   _____

2. If you found a $30.00 sweater at Marden's, how much would you pay for it?

   _____

3. If you bought 2 hairbrushes at Doogan's, how much would you pay?

   _____

4. When can you get the breakfast special at Jimmy's Diner?

   _____

5. If you rented a car from Rent a Wreck for three days and you traveled 30 miles each day, how much would you owe?

   _____

B Read the information and answer the questions below.

THAT'S MISLEADING!

Advertisers want to get your attention. They want to sell you something or make you do something. Sometimes, however, an advertisement is misleading. That means it gives you information that is not exactly true or is true only under certain conditions. For example, when an advertisement says that a certain food has "reduced fat," it only means that the food has less fat than the original food. The "reduced fat" food may still be high in fat. Saying that a food has "reduced fat" is a little misleading because it makes you think the food has just a little fat.

Have you ever seen one of those "before" and "after" advertisements? They sometimes show a photograph of someone before they lost weight and after they lost weight. These ads can be misleading too. They don't always show the same person in the "before" photograph and the "after" photograph.

The law protects consumers from some types of misleading advertising. For example, stores are not allowed to use the "bait and switch" sales technique. A store uses the "bait and switch" technique when it advertises a product on sale to get you to go to the store, but it doesn't actually have the product in the store. That's not legal.

1. What is the definition of a misleading ad?

_____

_____

2. What is the "bait and switch" sales technique?

_____

_____

3. If a store advertised something they didn't have, what would you do?

_____

_____

4. What is misleading about this bakery ad?

_____

_____

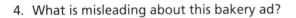

TAKE IT OUTSIDE: Look in a newspaper or magazine for advertisements that have misleading information. Bring your examples to class to share with your classmates.

2 LESSON

Are you an impulse shopper?

A Choose the correct form of the words to complete the questions below. Then answer the questions.

NOUN	VERB	ADJECTIVE
1. extension	extend	extensive
2. suspicion	suspect	suspicious
3. profit	profit	profitable
4. advertisement	advertise	XXXXX
5. selection	select	XXXXX
6. purchase	purchase	XXXXX
7. expiration	expire	XXXXX
8. impulse	XXXXX	impulsive

1. Why might a teacher _____ a class for a few minutes?

   _____

2. What would make you _____ that someone was lying?

   _____

3. What could you buy and then sell at a _____?

   _____

4. In addition to television, where can stores _____?

   _____

5. Which store in your area has the best _____ of fruits and vegetables?

   _____

6. Why might someone return a _____ to a store?

   _____

7. What should you do with unused medicine after its _____ date?

   _____

8. What was the last thing you bought on _____?

   _____

B Choose a word from the box to complete each sentence.

in bulk	ended up	time limit	extension	out of stock
expiration	brand	store credit	rain check	

1. She was planning to buy a car, but she _____ buying a truck.

2. My report was due this week, but my instructor gave me an _____ until next week.

3. What _____ of shampoo do you prefer?

4. It's not legal for a store to advertise something that is _____.

5. It is usually cheaper to buy things _____.

6. Is there a _____ for paying a credit card bill?

7. When you return something, most stores would rather give you _____ than cash.

8. You have to renew your driver's license before the _____ date.

C What could these people do? Write your ideas.

1. Xiao Li bought a sweater for his sister, but the sweater was too small. What do you think Xiao Li should do with the sweater?

_____

_____

2. Arturo saw an ad for a radio on sale at a nearby store. When he got to the store, however, there weren't any radios left. The salesclerk showed Arturo several more radios, but they were much more expensive. What could Arturo do?

_____

_____

3. Ken is an impulse shopper, especially when he goes shopping for food. He buys more food than his family can eat. What could Ken do to stop impulse shopping?

_____

_____

4. When Leila went shopping for some new clothes, the salesperson asked if she needed help. What could Leila say to the salesperson?

_____

_____

5. Cyndi's grandmother needs some new clothes, but it's difficult for her to go shopping. Cyndi offered to go shopping for her, but she doesn't want to buy anything her grandmother can't wear. What do you think Cyndi should do?

_____

_____

6. Don bought a new television set but after a month he started having problems with it. What do you think he should do?

_____

_____

85

3 LESSON

Do you have your receipt?

A Number each conversation in order starting with number #1.

Conversation A

_____ Yes, we do—as long as you have another form of identification.

_____ Yes, I'd like to pay for these.

_____ Yes. That would be fine.

_____ Okay. How would you like to pay for them?

___1___ Can I help you?

_____ Will a driver's license do?

_____ Do you take credit cards?

Conversation B

_____ Do you have your receipt?

___1___ Can I help you?

_____ Yes, I do. Here it is.

_____ I'd rather get cash back.

_____ Okay. I can give you store credit for that amount.

_____ Can I speak to the manager, please?

_____ Yes, of course.

_____ Yes, I'd like to return this.

_____ I'm sorry but we only give store credit.

Conversation C

_____ Yes, of course. They come with a two year warranty.

___1___ Can I help you?

_____ That's correct. But you can also buy an extended warranty.

_____ Yes, can you tell me what the warranty is on the television sets?

_____ But it's only $5 a month. Really, it's a very good deal.

_____ Did you say two years?

_____ No thank you. I'll take the television set, but I'm not interested in an extended warranty.

_____ No thank you. I'm not interested in an extended warranty.

Conversation D

_____ And how would you like to pay for that?

_____ Yes, you have 30 days to return something.

_____ Yes, of course. But be sure to bring the receipt with you.

___1___ Can I help you?

_____ Is there a time limit?

_____ Yes. Can I bring this back if it doesn't fit my husband?

_____ Can I get cash back?

_____ That's good. I'll take this then.

_____ Yes, of course. You can make an exchange or a return.

_____ By cash.

B Complete these sentences.

1. If a store accepts only cash or credit card, you cannot pay by _____

2. If something is nonreturnable, you can't _____

3. If you lose the receipt for something you purchased, you can't _____

4. If a salesperson tries to pressure you into buying something, you can _____

5. If something comes with a warranty, you can _____

6. If you buy things in bulk, you can _____

7. If something is advertised "on sale" but is out of stock, you can _____

8. If you can't find something in a store, you should _____

C Read the information and complete the sentences below.

> ### How are you going to pay for it?
>
> When you decide to buy something, there are a number of different ways you can pay for it. You can always pay by cash, but that means you have to carry around a lot of money. Instead of cash, you can purchase some things by writing a personal check. To do this, however, you have to open a checking account at a bank. You also have to make sure you always have enough money in your account to cover your purchases.
>
> Some stores will also give you a charge account. This allows you to "charge" or purchase things using your charge card. Every month the store sends you a bill for the things you bought. For some charge accounts you must pay the full amount at the end of the month. Some charge accounts, however, will allow you to make a minimum monthly payment. You only have to pay part of the bill at the end of the month, but you also have to pay interest on the amount of money you owe. Credit cards are another popular tool for buying things. Most credit cards allow you to make a minimum monthly payment, but they also charge a high interest rate.
>
> Many stores also have layaway programs. If you don't have enough money to buy something, for example a new couch, you can put it on layaway. You make a down payment and the store holds the item for you. Then, usually over the next 30 to 90 days, you can pay the rest of the money.

1. One disadvantage of using cash to buy things is that _____

2. If you want to pay by personal check, you must _____

3. Credit card companies make money by _____

4. If you want to put something on layaway, you must first make _____

5. One advantage of using a layaway program to buy something is that _____

4 LESSON

Best Buys

A Answer the questions.

1. A gallon of soap costs $4.50 while a quart of the same soap costs $1.75. How much money can you save by buying a gallon of soap instead of 4 quarts? _____

2. A package of 16 rolls of toilet papers sells for $4.80 while a package of 4 rolls sells for $2.00. How much can you save by buying one package of 16 rolls instead of 4 packages of 4 rolls? _____

3. How much cheaper is it to buy a half-gallon of juice for $3.60 than 2 quarts of juice at $2.20 each? _____

4. A 16-ounce bottle of shampoo sells for $6.00 while an 8-ounce bottle of the same shampoo sells for $4.25. How much money can you save by buying the 16-ounce bottle instead of two 8-ounce bottles? _____

5. A weekly magazine costs $4.00 an issue if you buy it at a newsstand. However, if you buy a subscription to the magazine, it costs $46.00 a year. How much money can you save in a year by buying a subscription? _____

B Read the online Consumer Opinion on page 89 and the statements below. Check (✓) *True* or *False*.

	True	False
1. The writer is giving an opinion about the Eton 7-Cup Rice Cooker.	☐	☐
2. The writer gave a high overall rating to this cooker.	☐	☐
3. The writer thinks the rice cooker is hard to clean.	☐	☐
4. The writer advises people to buy this brand of rice cooker.	☐	☐
5. The writer couldn't read the instruction booklet that came with the rice cooker.	☐	☐
6. The instructions that came with the rice cooker were incorrect.	☐	☐
7. The rice cooker doesn't cook rice correctly.	☐	☐
8. The rice cooker doesn't have a heat timer.	☐	☐
9. The heat timer on the rice cooker doesn't work.	☐	☐
10. The heat timer could cause a fire.	☐	☐
11. The rice cooker is convenient to use.	☐	☐
12. The company provides good service to its customers.	☐	☐

Consumer Opinions

•CARS •BOOKS •MUSIC •ELECTRONICS •HOME & GARDEN •OFFICE SUPPLY

- ◉ Home
- ◉ Log In
- ◉ Contact Us
- ◉ E-mail
- ◉ Newsletter
- ◉ Shop Smart
- ◉ Product Recalls
- ◉ Discussions
- ◉ Consumer Protection

Search for [   ]   Rice Cookers

Eton 7-Cup Rice Cooker

Overall rating: ★ ☆ ☆ ☆ ☆

Ease of Use: ★ ☆ ☆ ☆ ☆
Durability: ★ ★ ☆ ☆ ☆
Ease of Cleaning: ★ ★ ★ ☆ ☆

Pros
Not too hard to clean.

Cons
The instructions are wrong and the heat timer doesn't always work.

Reviewer's Advice
This isn't a good rice cooker. Buy a different brand. If you do buy this brand, be sure to save the box and the receipt.

Full Review
I had problems with the rice cooker from the very first time I used it. The instruction booklet tells you to use one cup of water per one cup of rice. When I did this, the rice came out hard and burned. I tried again using 1 1/2 cups of water per 1 cup of rice. After cooking the rice for the correct amount of time, the rice at the top was edible, but the rice at the bottom of the cooker was burned. I tried again using 2 cups of water per cup of rice and that worked just about right. The company should provide the correct cooking instructions. Customers shouldn't have to figure it out.

Besides the incorrect instructions, this rice cooker doesn't cook evenly. No matter what you do, the rice at the top cooks at a different rate than the rice at the bottom. This shouldn't happen.

A third serious problem with this rice cooker is that the heat timer doesn't always work. The heat timer has two positions. You press it down for cooking the rice and up for keeping the rice warm. To cook the rice, you put the water and rice in the cooker and press the heat timer down. After about 15 minutes, the cooking cycle is supposed to be finished and the heat timer is supposed to pop up to the "keep warm" position. With this rice cooker, however, the heat timer doesn't always pop up to the "keep warm" position. Instead, the rice keeps cooking. That could be dangerous. It also means you must keep watching the rice and time it yourself.

I sent an email to the company's website explaining the problem, but they never answered me. Unfortunately, I have already thrown out the box it came in as well as my receipt so I can't ask for a refund.

5
LESSON

That's really expensive, isn't it?

A Add the correct tag to each statement on the right. Write the tag on the line.

1. He didn't like it, _____?   a. can she
2. That was a profitable business, _____?   b. isn't it
3. He speaks Spanish very well, _____?   c. was it
4. That's the end of the movie, _____?   d. do they
5. Shoes cost a lot, _____?   e. is it
6. It wasn't very cold yesterday, _____?   f. did he
7. She can't sing very well, _____?   g. didn't he
8. Clothes from thrift stores don't cost a lot, _____?   h. wasn't it
9. That dress isn't very pretty, _____?   i. don't they
10. He certainly left in a hurry, _____?   j. doesn't he

B Add tag questions to complete the conversations.

1. A: This is a great movie, _____?
   B: It sure is. The beginning was scary though, _____?
   A: Absolutely. I couldn't believe it.

2. A: This grapefruit is really sour, _____?
   B: It sure is.

3. A: There certainly wasn't much to eat at the party, _____?
   B: No, there wasn't. I'm still hungry.

4. A: She couldn't sing very well tonight, _____?
   B: No, she couldn't. She's usually much better.

5. A: He hit the floor hard, _____?
   B: He certainly did. I can't believe he didn't break any bones.

6. A: She spoke very well, _____?
   B: Yes, she did. She always does.

C Agree with each tag question below.

1. A: Shakespeare was a great writer, wasn't he?

   B: _____

2. A: This is great music, isn't it?

   B: _____

3. A: Mexican food is delicious, isn't it?

   B: _____

4. A: It's not easy to learn a new language, is it?

   B: _____

5. A: Email is really fast, isn't it?

   B: _____

6. A: It wasn't very cold yesterday, was it?

   B: _____

William Shakespeare (1564–1616)

D Disagree with each tag question below.

1. A: English is a really easy language, isn't it?

   B: _____

2. A: Impulse buying can save you a lot of money, can't it?

   B: _____

3. A: It's stupid to buy things in bulk, isn't it?

   B: _____

E Complete these tag questions with your own opinions.

1. _____ is really delicious, _____ ?

2. _____ is a lot of fun, _____ ?

3. _____ was a great actor, _____ ?

4. _____ isn't good for you, _____ ?

5. _____ is really delicious, _____ ?

WORK

LESSON

Do you sell greeting cards?

A Study the store floor plan below and circle the best answer.

1. Paint supplies are next to the _____.

   A. entrance
   B. pet supplies
   C. plumbing supplies

2. Pens and pencils are probably in _____.

   A. aisle 2
   B. aisle 3
   C. aisle 4

3. You can find a needle and thread in the section behind _____.

   A. garden and yard supplies
   B. sewing supplies
   C. sports equipment

4. If you need oil for your car, you should go to aisle _____.

   A. 4
   B. 6
   C. 7

5. The _____ is near the entrance of the store.

   A. sports equipment
   B. information desk
   C. checkout counter

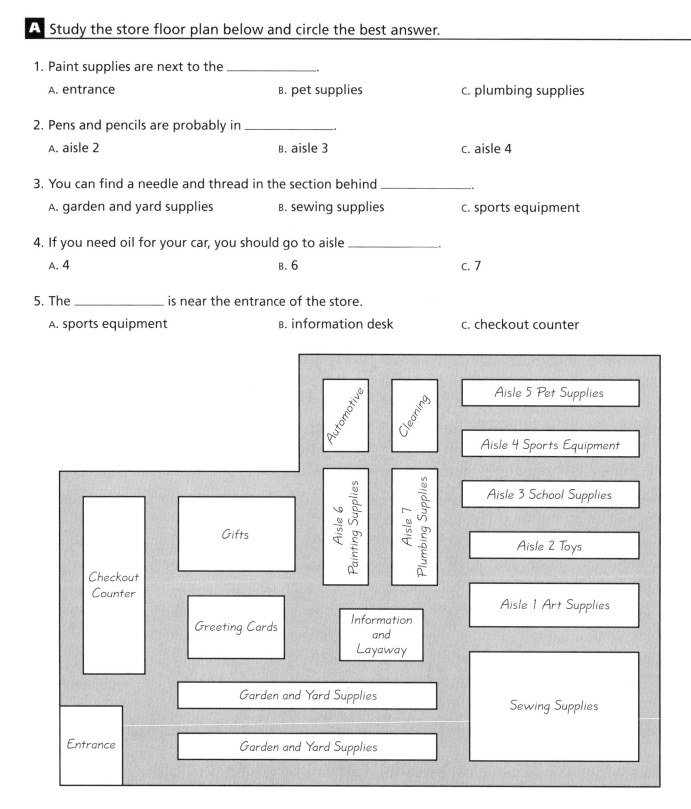

B A customer and a store clerk are standing at the Information Desk of the store in Activity 1. Use the floor plan to complete the conversations below. Circle the best answer.

1. Customer: I'm looking for scissors.

   Clerk: Scissors? They are in with _____. (sewing supplies / sports equipment) That's behind the garden and yard supplies.

2. Customer: Do you sell brooms?

   Clerk: Yes, we do. They're in with _____ supplies. (pet / cleaning) That's aisle 7. Just go down that way past the _____ supplies. (automotive / plumbing)

3. Customer: Do you sell fishing rods?

   Clerk: Yes, we do. They are in aisle _____. (3 / 4) Just go down past the plumbing supplies on your left and you'll see the _____ on your right just after school supplies. (toys / sports equipment)

4. Customer: Do you carry those things to put paint on walls?

   Clerk: Do you mean a paint brush?

   Customer: Yes, a paint brush.

   Clerk: You'll find them just over there in aisle _____. (6 / 7)

5. Customer: Do you carry vacuum cleaner bags?

   Clerk: Yes, we do. They are at the end of aisle _____ in the cleaning supplies. (3 / 7)

   Customer: Thanks.

   Clerk: You're welcome.

6. Customer: Do you sell hoses?

   Clerk: Sure. They're in _____ supplies. They're at the end of the aisle near the entrance. (sewing / garden and yard)

   Customer: Thanks.

7. Customer: Can you tell me where the wrapping paper is?

   Clerk: Sure. It's in the gift section, next to the _____. (painting supplies / pet supplies)

8. Customer: Do you sell children's clothes?

   Clerk: _____. (Yes, we do. / No, I'm sorry, we don't.)

★ ★

TAKE IT OUTSIDE: Visit a store in your area that sells a variety of things. Study the organization of the store and draw a simple floor plan. Then share your floor plan with your classmates and answer any questions they have.

★ ★

Where can I get help?

A Use the list of Resources for Consumers below to answer these questions.

1. Which resource provides information about different types of insurance? _____

2. Which 3 resources are U.S. federal government agencies? _____ _____

   _____

3. Which federal agency would handle a complaint about false advertising? _____

4. What does the acronym HUD stand for? _____

5. How could you file a complaint with the FTC? _____

6. How can you get in touch with the ACLU? _____

Resources for Consumers

Consumers can get help from federal and state government agencies and from the many consumer advocacy groups. Here are just a few of the available resources:

The American Civil Liberties Union (ACLU)

The American Civil Liberties Union focuses on issues affecting individual freedom. To contact them, call a local ACLU office listed in your telephone directory.

Attorneys General

If you have a consumer issue involving the laws of your state, contact your state attorney general.

Better Business Bureaus (BBB)

The Council of Better Business Bureaus has more than 100 local offices nationwide. Check out a business or find out about the dispute resolution program. Look in your telephone book for the nearest BBB.

The Federal Communications Commission (FCC)

The Federal Communications Commission oversees interstate and international communications by radio, television, wire, satellite, and cable. To make a complaint or obtain information, call 888-CALL-FCC.

The Federal Trade Commission (FTC)

The Federal Trade Commission is responsible for enforcing numerous consumer protection laws focusing on deceptive and unfair trade practices.

To file a complaint or obtain information, call 877-FTC-HELP.

The U.S. Department of Housing and Urban Development (HUD)

The U.S. Department of Housing and Urban Development is responsible for handling complaints regarding housing discrimination, manufactured housing, and land sales.

INSURE.COM

This website provides consumer information and resources on life, health, car, and home insurance topics.

NOLO.COM

Nolo provides legal information for consumers on many different consumer topics; 800-728-3555.

Public Citizen

Founded by Ralph Nader, Public Citizen is a consumer advocacy organization that promotes consumer interest in energy, environment, trade, health, and government issues.

From "Resources for Consumers" from *Understanding Consumer Rights* by Nicolette Parsi and Marc Robinson, New York: Dorling Kindersley, 2000.

B Read about each person below and answer the questions.

1. Sylvia found an apartment she liked but as soon as the owner of the building learned that she had young children, he said the apartment was no longer available. Which of the resources on page 94 could she get help from? _____

2. James found a roofing company to put a new roof on his house, but he doesn't know if it does good work. Which of the resources on page 94 could he use to get information about the roofing company? _____

3. Fatima bought a toaster oven from a hardware store in her town. When she got home, she found that it didn't work. Now the store refuses to take it back. Which of the resources on page 94 could she get help from? _____

C Choose the correct form of the words to complete the sentences below.

VERB	NOUN
1. complain	complaint
2. protect	protection
3. discriminate	discrimination
4. inform	information
5. organize	organization

1. You have the right to _____ if you buy something that doesn't work. You can send a letter of _____ to the FTC.

2. The goal of the ACLU is to _____ the freedom of individuals.

3. _____ because of your age is illegal in the U.S.

4. Nolo can _____ you about many different legal issues.

5. The BBB is an _____ that gives useful information about businesses in your area.

★ ★

TAKE IT OUTSIDE: Talk to several people you know. Ask them the questions below.

1. Have you ever had a problem with a store or a business?

2. What was the problem?

3. What did you do?

★ ★

TAKE IT ONLINE: Use your favorite search engine to look for information about HUD or the FTC. List 3 interesting things you learn on the website.

1. _____

2. _____

3. _____

REVIEW

LESSON

Practice Test

A Read the price chart below to answer the next 6 questions. Use the Answer Sheet.

Type of Food	Store A	Store B	Store C	Store D
Produce	$50.00	$52.50	$48.90	$53.10
Dairy Products	36.80	41.50	37.00	37.50
Grain / Cereals	52.50	50.99	53.00	52.40
Processed Food	50.50	54.80	52.50	55.00
Meat	50.00	49.50	52.00	52.50
Cleaning Supplies	61.00	59.00	65.50	62.40

1. Which store has the most expensive produce?
   A. Store A
   B. Store B
   C. Store C
   D. Store D

2. Which store should you go to for the cheapest cleaning supplies?
   A. Store A
   B. Store B
   C. Store C
   D. Store D

3. Which store probably has the cheapest milk?
   A. Store A
   B. Store B
   C. Store C
   D. Store D

4. If you spend $59.00 on cleaning supplies at Store B, how much more will you spend to buy the same products at Store C?
   A. $65.50
   B. $5.50
   C. $6.50
   D. $61.00

5. If you spend $54.80 for processed food at Store B, how much will you spend at Store D?
   A. $50.50
   B. $53.10
   C. $61.00
   D. $55.00

6. What is more expensive at Store A than at Store C?
   A. Produce
   B. Dairy Products
   C. Meat
   D. Cleaning Supplies

ANSWER SHEET

1	A	B	C	D
2	A	B	C	D
3	A	B	C	D
4	A	B	C	D
5	A	B	C	D
6	A	B	C	D
7	A	B	C	D
8	A	B	C	D
9	A	B	C	D
10	A	B	C	D

B Use the information below to answer the next 4 questions. Use the Answer Sheet on page 96.

Examples of Misleading Ads for Telephone Service

Telephone Company A advertised long-distance calls for only 5 cents per minute. However, the company did not say clearly in its ads that there was also a $7.95 monthly fee.

Telephone Company B advertised long-distance calls for only 5 cents per minute. However, the company didn't say that there was a minimum charge of $1 for every call, even if it was a short call.

---

7. If you had your telephone service with Company A and you used the phone for only one minute during the month, how much would you pay?

A. 7 cents

B. 70 cents

C. $7.95

D. $8.00

8. If you had your telephone service with Company A and you used the phone for 300 minutes in one month, how much would you pay?

A. $157.95

B. $22.95

C. $150.00

D. $15.00

9. If you had your telephone service with Company B and you used the phone for only one minute during the month, how much would you pay?

A. 5 cents

B. $1.00

C. $1.05

D. $100.00

10. If you had your telephone service with Company B, which statement below would be true?

A. A five-minute call is cheaper than a ten-minute call.

B. A twenty-minute call is as expensive as a thirty-minute call.

C. A one-minute call and a twenty-minute call cost the same.

D. A five-minute call costs 25 cents.

HOW DID YOU DO? Count the number of correct answers on your answer sheet. Record this number in the bar graph on the inside back cover.

Spotlight: Reading

A Unscramble the questions below. Then use the picture to answer them.

1. have / do / you / financing

   Customer: _____

   Salesperson: _____

2. here / sell / can / my car / for cash / I

   Customer: _____

   Salesperson: _____

3. for sale / have / do you / any trucks

   Customer: _____

   Salesperson: _____

4. any / your cars / a warranty / do / come with / of

   Customer: _____

   Salesperson: _____

B Read the article. Use context to guess the meaning of the boldfaced words. Then match each boldfaced word with a synonym below. Write the synonym on the line.

CAR DEALER CITED FOR FALSE ADVERTISING

Franklin Auto in Fredericksburg has agreed to **reform** its business practices. The dealership was accused last November of failing to honor advertised prices and refusing to **refund** deposits.

Customers were **lured** into the dealership with advertisements of extremely low prices for cars. In its ads, however, the dealership did not say that the low prices were only available to buyers who **financed** a loan through the dealership at a very high interest rate.

When customers **expressed** interest in a car, they were **pressured** to leave a deposit for the car while a credit check was done. Later, when customers learned about the expensive financing that came with the advertised price of the car, many tried to **cancel** their purchase. The dealership, however, **refused** to return their deposit.

---

1. reform _____   a. said no

2. refund _____   b. forced

3. lured _____   c. change

4. financed _____   d. attracted

5. expressed _____   e. give back

6. pressured _____   f. got money for

7. cancel _____   g. stop

8. refused _____   h. showed

C Reread the article in Activity B. Then decide if the statements below are *True* or *False*. Circle your answer.

1. Franklin Auto offered very low prices to all its customers.	TRUE	FALSE
2. To get a low price on a car, customers had to finance a loan through Franklin Auto.	TRUE	FALSE
3. Franklin Auto charged a very low interest rate for its loans.	TRUE	FALSE
4. Customers didn't know about the expensive financing before they put a deposit on the car.	TRUE	FALSE
5. When customers decided to cancel their purchases, Franklin Auto gave them back their deposit.	TRUE	FALSE
6. Franklin Auto treated people unfairly.	TRUE	FALSE

Spotlight: Writing

A Give a reason to complete each sentence below.

1. I want to return this television set because _____

2. I was unhappy with the service at your store because _____

3. The main reason I am returning this coat is that _____

4. I've decided to return this computer because _____

5. I'd like to return this coffee maker; it _____

B Complete the story. Write the correct form of the verbs below.

About a month ago my friend Shirin _____ (1) to buy
3 things from a mail order catalogue. She called the 800 number on
the back of the catalogue and a sales representative _____
(2) her order. The three things she ordered were a red sweater, a black
jacket, and a white shirt. A week later a package _____
(3) from the store, but the contents weren't exactly what Shirin was
expecting. Instead of a red sweater, the store _____ (4) a blue
sweater. They mailed the right jacket, but when Shirin _____
(5) it on, the zipper wouldn't go up or down. The white shirt was the
right color and it _____ (6) just right, but after Shirin washed
the shirt, it _____ (7) two sizes too small.

(1) decide

(2) take

(3) arrive

(4) send

(5) try

(6) fit

(7) be

C Complete the return form below. Use information from the story in Activity B.

DARBY'S RETURN/EXCHANGE

GUARANTEED 100%
NO QUESTIONS. NO EXCEPTIONS.

1 Name	Phone
Shirin Hamadi	(561) 555-4993

Street	City	State	Zip
543 Bennett St. Apt. 4A	Delray Beach	Florida	33446

2 DESCRIBE REASON(S) Please describe the problem(s) as specifically as possible so that we can improve our products for you. Your input here makes a big difference.

_____

_____

_____

REASON CODES Use one code to explain why you are returning item(s). Please describe the problem(s) in detail above.

APPAREL	SERVICE	QUALITY	SATISFACTION
14 Too small	18 Wrong item sent	22 Defective	26 Did not like color
15 Too short	19 Duplicate ship	23 Didn't like fabric	27 Did not like style
16 Too large	20 Damaged	24 Shrunk	28 Item not as described
17 Too long	21 Arrived too late	25 Poor quality	29 Item not as pictured

3 ITEMS YOU ARE RETURNING Please list any items that you are returning. Be sure to include one reason code for each item from the "Reason Codes" in Section 2.

Reason Code	Qty.	Item #	Description	Size	Color	Price
		075	sweater	M		$28.00
		862	jacket	M		$37.00
		407	shirt	M		$16.50

UNIT 6: Rules and Laws

LESSON 1

She has jury duty.

A Look at the photo below. Identify the people.

1.

2.

3.

4.

5.

B Look at the photo above. Check (✓) *True* or *False*.

	True	False
1. The witness is a man.	☐	☐
2. The attorney is showing a photo of tire marks to the judge.	☐	☐
3. Jury members can see information on computers.	☐	☐
4. This case involves battery and disturbing the peace.	☐	☐
5. The testimony probably involves a traffic accident.	☐	☐

C Read the newspaper article about the trial. Answer the questions below in complete sentences.

Harris Trial in Second Day
Witness: "I was terrified!"

The trial of James Harris continued today as jurors heard witness testimony about the hit-and-run accident.

Lynn Rogers described how Harris ran a red light and hit the passenger side of her car, then drove off into busy commuter traffic.

"I was terrified," Rogers testified. "I'm just so thankful that my family wasn't in the car when he hit me."

Rogers told the packed courtroom that seconds after she was hit, she saw Harris crash into another vehicle a couple hundred yards away.

"It was horrible," Rogers said. "I thought someone might have been hurt, so I immediately called 911." The police and paramedics arrived quickly and took Harris into custody, after treating him for minor injuries.

Jurors appeared visibly upset as they viewed photos of the crash scene.

---

1. What is the name of the defendant?

_____

2. Who is the witness?

_____

3. Why is the defendant on trial?

_____

4. Using the context clues, what do you think a *hit-and-run accident* is?

_____

_____

D Summarize the newspaper article.

_____

_____

_____

_____

_____

_____

2 LESSON

It's a felony.

A Write the correct form of the words to complete the sentences.

1. If you _____ a law, you might be arrested. (violation/violate)

2. For serious crimes, you may face _____ of up to 20 years. (imprisonment/imprison)

3. The _____ for misdemeanors is less than one year in prison. (punishment/punish)

4. If you are _____ of a crime, you will have a criminal record. (conviction/convicted)

5. You should make a report to the police if you are the victim of a _____. (robbery/rob)

6. If someone is killed during the _____ of a felony, you will face additional charges. (commission/commit)

7. He _____ the police officer, and so he was arrested. (offense/offended)

8. The jury voted to _____ the defendant on a misdemeanor rather than a felony. (conviction/convict)

9. _____ is a crime against property, rather than directly against a person. (burglary/burglarize)

10. Writing on walls is a type of _____. (vandalism/vandalize)

B Write a sentence about each photo using a word from Activity A.

1. _____

2. _____

C Look at the bar graph. Circle the correct answers to the questions below.

Source: http://www.ojp.usdoj.gov/

1. In which region of the United States is the rate of assault the greatest?

   A. the Northeast   C. the South

   B. the Midwest   D. the West

2. Where is there the lowest incidence of robberies?

   A. the Northeast   C. the South

   B. the Midwest   D. the West

3. Which region has the fewest rapes or sexual assaults?

   A. the Northeast   C. the South

   B. the Midwest   D. the West

4. Which region is the safest overall in terms of these violent crimes?

   A. the Northeast   C. the South

   B. the Midwest   D. the West

5. Which region is the most dangerous?

   A. the Northeast   C. the South

   B. the Midwest   D. the West

3
LESSON

To hear this message again, press 9.

A Unscramble the words to write sentences.

1. the Marriage License Division / reached / have / you

_____

2. required / premarital / are / physicals / not

_____

3. it is issued / valid / is / for 60 days thereafter / the marriage license / on the day / and

_____

_____

4. $50 / the cost / in cash / is

_____

5. processed / applications / are / from 8:30 to 4:00

_____

6. to complete / take / 45 minutes / approximately / it will / the application process

_____

_____

7. on the application / your social security number / have / must / you

_____

8. bring / your date of birth / you must / a valid driver's license / or photo ID / with

_____

B Complete the telephone conversation with information from Activity A.

1. A. Do I need to have a physical exam before I can get a marriage license?

   B. _____

2. A. How long will it take to get the license?

   B. _____

3. A. So do you think I will be finished in half an hour?

   B. _____

4. A: What are the hours?

   B. _____

5. A. Did you say it would cost $75?

   B. _____

6. A. I don't have a driver's license. What should I do?

   B. _____

C Paraphrase the following statements.

1. If you are between the ages of 18 and 21, you must present a valid driver's license or photo ID, and a certified birth certificate.

   _____

   _____

2. You must complete driver's education before you can take the test to get a learner's permit.

   _____

   _____

3. A permit is required to deposit garbage at the county dump site.

   _____

   _____

4. Recyclables, such as glass bottles and aluminum containers, may be brought in to the recycling center without a permit and are free of charge as long as they are kept separate from trash.

   _____

   _____

   _____

What to do when you're arrested.

LESSON 4

A Read the questions in the chart below and write your guesses in column 2.

1 Questions	2 My guesses before reading the text	3 Answers from the text
a) What rights do people have when they are arrested?		
b) How should a person behave when arrested?		
c) What can people do if they can't afford to pay a lawyer?		

B Read the information below and look for answers to the questions in Activity A. Write the answers in column 3 of the chart.

What You Should Do if You're Arrested

Act Thoughtfully

Don't argue with the arresting officer. Keep your hands visible and don't move suddenly. What you say and do can be used against you, so be respectful and polite. Stay calm. If the arrest is a mistake, you can sort it out later. The important thing is to stay in control.

Know Your Rights

Everyone has rights when they are arrested. The arresting officer should read you your rights. These rights include the right to remain silent and the right to a lawyer. You do not have to say anything until you are represented by an attorney. You should be able to make a phone call.

Get a Lawyer

It's always wise to have legal representation when you have been arrested. Your attorney can advise you on what you should do. If you can't afford your own attorney, a judge will appoint one for you that will provide services for free. Legal aid services also provide low-cost representation to clients with little money.

C Check (✓) *True* or *False*.

	True	False
1. Only citizens have rights when they are arrested.	❏	❏
2. You should protest to the officer if you think the arrest is unfair.	❏	❏
3. You must answer police questions when arrested.	❏	❏
4. If you don't have any money, you can get a lawyer for free.	❏	❏
5. Only guilty people need lawyers.	❏	❏
6. Legal aid services are often available at little or no cost.	❏	❏

D Answer the following questions.

1. Why do you think some people don't call a lawyer when they are arrested?

_____

_____

2. What mistakes do you think people might make when they are stopped by the police?

_____

_____

3. Why do you think it is important to move slowly and keep your hands visible?

_____

_____

E Write a summary of the article.

_____

_____

_____

_____

_____

_____

_____

_____

_____

5 LESSON

It shows the amount that you must pay.

A Combine the following sentences using an adjective clause.

EXAMPLE: The student left early. He forgot his book.
The student who left early forgot his book.

1. The house was painted last month. It caught fire yesterday.

   _____

2. Jaime bought a new car. It was a great buy.

   _____

3. A man witnessed the robbery. He is testifying today at the trial.

   _____

4. A young girl was killed in the accident. She was walking home from school.

   _____

5. A lot of people don't vote. They complain about the government anyway.

   _____

B Read the situation and look at the photo. Write 4 sentences using adjective clauses.

   Yesterday you were walking to the parking lot at school when you saw this man. He broke into a car and drove off in it. The police want you to describe as much as you can.

   _____

   _____

   _____

   _____

   _____

   _____

   _____

   _____

   _____

C Read the letter. Write *who, that, which,* or X (if no pronoun is needed) on the lines.

Dear Linda,

You'll never believe what happened! Remember I told you about the guy Rick _____ (1) works at the desk next to me? Well, he asked me to go to a nightclub _____ (2) just opened a week ago. Lots of people _____ (3) I know from work went too. Anyway, we had been there about an hour when we decided to leave to get something to eat. We wanted to go to a new restaurant downtown _____ (4) opened a few months ago. We went to the parking garage, but Rick's truck wasn't there! We spoke to the man _____ (5) was working there and he said that he saw a blue pick-up truck leave thirty minutes earlier. Rick used a cell phone _____ (6) another person in the garage had to call 911. Two police officers came and Rick _____ (7) filed a report with them. By this time it was getting late and I wanted to go home. We asked the police about transportation, but they said the bus _____ (8) goes by there only operates until 9:00 P.M. So we had to take a taxi, _____ (9) was expensive.

The next day Rick got a call from one of the police officers _____ (10) said she had found his truck. You'll never believe where she found it—in the parking garage. We were sure we had parked on the 4th floor, but I guess we had actually parked on the 5th floor. Rick was so embarrassed _____ (11) he didn't talk to me at all the next week. I finally spoke with him this week and _____ (12) we made plans to go out again. This time I'm driving!

—Mila

D Answer the questions about you. Use adjective clauses in your answer.

1. What person has influenced you the most?

   _____

   _____

2. What do you think is the most serious public safety problem?

   _____

   _____

3. What do you think contributes to crime?

   _____

   _____

Laws protect children.

A Read questions 1 to 3. Then read the information below and answer the questions.

1. How did the boy misbehave?

   _____

2. How did his parents punish him?

   _____

3. Why do the parents now have a record of suspected child abuse?

   _____

QUESTION

My family came from India five years ago. My son's friends at school were bad boys who told him to miss school and stay out late. My husband and I grew tired of this behavior, and locked our son in his room for two days. His teacher learned about his punishment and reported us for child abuse. Someone came to our house to investigate. Even though the investigation has ended, we still have a record of suspected[1] child abuse. Why did this happen?

ANSWER

American laws give parents a lot of freedom on how to discipline their children. But the laws also protect children if the authorities believe that the discipline becomes dangerous. The government strictly enforces these laws against child abuse and child neglect[2]. These laws are meant to protect the safety of children, even if the parents do not mean to hurt the children. You need to understand how the American laws affect how you raise your children, and you may have to learn new ways to discipline your children.

The U.S. laws are based on the views of the general American society, which may be different from your own views. It does not matter how people in your home country use discipline. You will be judged by the customs of America and not by your own personal religious or cultural beliefs. Your best protection is to know the law. Once a child abuse report is made, the process can take weeks, months, or even years to end. You may have to go to court. The government can even take your children away from your home *before* you go to court.

---
[1] suspected: not yet proven
[2] neglect: failure to provide proper care

From *Understanding the Laws On How You Can Discipline Your Children* by Lydia Fan, The Coalition for Asian American Children and Families, January 2002. Reprinted by permission.

B Read the sentences and check (✓) *True* or *False*.

	True	False
1. U.S. laws allow parents to use any form of discipline.	❑	❑
2. The government rarely enforces laws against child abuse.	❑	❑
3. A teacher can report a suspected case of child abuse.	❑	❑
4. The way your parents disciplined you may not be legal in the U.S.	❑	❑
5. You may have to go to court if you are accused of child neglect.	❑	❑

C There are many forms of child abuse and child neglect. Group these examples in the chart below.

burning

failing to send to school

failing to take to the doctor

not feeding properly

kicking

shaking

shaming

slapping

name calling

not using a child seat for a baby in a car

Physical Abuse	Emotional Abuse	Neglect

★ ★

TAKE IT OUTSIDE: Ask 3 friends the questions below and write their answers. Then share what you learned from your classmates.

Person's first name	What is one example of child abuse?	What is one example of child neglect?

★ ★

TAKE IT ONLINE: Go to your favorite search engine and enter the words "laws about child neglect." List 3 sites that give information about this topic.

1. _____

2. _____

3. _____

WORK

LESSON

Laws protect workers.

A Read the questions in the chart below and write your guesses in column 2.

1 Questions	2 My guesses before reading the text	3 Answers from the text
a) Twenty-five-year-old Sandra is a cashier in a large store. Last week her boss asked her to help unpack boxes in the storeroom. Sandra doesn't think she should have to do this because it's not in her job description. Is she right?		
b) Fong works from Wednesday through Sunday. A friend told him that he should get extra pay when he works on the weekend. Is his friend correct?		
c) Selena earns $10.00 an hour and last week she worked for 45 hours. How much money should her employer pay her for the week?		
d) Twelve-year-old Jesse wants to earn some money so she can take dance lessons. What types of work can she do?		
e) Sixteen-year-old Andy is trying to save money for college. What types of jobs can he do?		

B Read the information below and look for answers to the questions in Activity A. Then write the answers in column 3 of the chart on page 114.

Can an employee be required to do work that is not in the employee's job description?
Yes. The Fair Labor Standards Act (FLSA) does not limit the types of work employees age 18 and older may be asked to do. However, there are limits on the types of work that employees under the age of 18 can do.

Is extra pay required for weekend or night work?
Employers are not required to pay employees extra when they work on weekends or nights. The Fair Labor Standards Act (FLSA) does not require extra pay for weekend or night work. However, the FLSA does require that covered, nonexempt workers be paid not less than time and one-half the employee's regular rate for time worked over 40 hours in a workweek.

When must breaks and meal periods be given?
The Fair Labor Standards Act (FLSA) does not require breaks or meal periods be given to workers. Some states may have requirements for breaks or meal periods. If you work in a state which does not require breaks or meal periods, these benefits are a matter of agreement between the employer and the employee (or the employee's representative).

What is the youngest age at which a person can be employed?
The Fair Labor Standards Act (FLSA) sets 14 as the minimum age for most non-agricultural work. However, at any age, youth may deliver newspapers; perform in radio, television, movie, or theatrical productions; work in businesses owned by their parents (except in mining, manufacturing, or hazardous jobs); and perform babysitting or perform minor chores around a private home. Also, at any age, youth may be employed as homeworkers to gather evergreens and make evergreen wreaths. Different age requirements apply to the employment of youth in agriculture. Many states have enacted child labor laws, some of which may have a minimum age for employment which is higher than the FLSA. Where both the FLSA and state child labor laws apply, the higher minimum standard must be obeyed.

Source: http://www.dol.gov

 TAKE IT ONLINE: Use your favorite search engine to look for your state's requirements for breaks and meal periods. Summarize what you learn on the lines below.

_____

_____

_____

_____

Practice Test

DIRECTIONS: Read the article to answer the next 5 questions. Use the Answer Sheet.

Speed Laws

In this state, residential and business zones are 30 miles per hour unless otherwise posted. School zones are 15 miles per hour unless otherwise posted. This speed limit is observed 30 minutes before to 30 minutes after school is in session.

Maximum safe speed on highways is 55 miles per hour. Certain limited access highways may have a posted limit of 65 or 70 mph in specific areas. However, unless posted, you should observe a speed limit of no more than 55 mph.

Your maximum safe driving speed is always determined by the road and weather conditions. The posted speed limit is the maximum speed that is ever allowed, and it may not be appropriate for all conditions. You can get a speeding ticket for driving at the posted limit if conditions are unsafe, for example in snow, rain, or ice.

Fines will be doubled if there are constructions workers in a work zone, or if children are present in a school zone.

---

1. When should you drive <u>below</u> the speed limit?

   A. when it is snowing
   B. when the road is in bad condition
   C. when you can't see
   D. all of the above

2. What is the usual speed limit on highways?

   A. 65
   B. 70
   C. 55
   D. 35

3. When do you have to pay twice as much in fines?

   A. when workers or children are present in the zone
   B. when you go twice the speed limit
   C. when the conditions are unsafe
   D. when you are on the highway

4. What is the speed limit in residential zones?

   A. 55 mph
   B. 30 mph
   C. 15 mph
   D. 60 mph

5. Under what condition do you have to drive 15 mph in a school zone?

   A. in bad weather
   B. at night
   C. 30 minutes before school to 30 minutes after school is over
   D. all the time

ANSWER SHEET

	A	B	C	D
1	Ⓐ	Ⓑ	Ⓒ	Ⓓ
2	Ⓐ	Ⓑ	Ⓒ	Ⓓ
3	Ⓐ	Ⓑ	Ⓒ	Ⓓ
4	Ⓐ	Ⓑ	Ⓒ	Ⓓ
5	Ⓐ	Ⓑ	Ⓒ	Ⓓ
6	Ⓐ	Ⓑ	Ⓒ	Ⓓ
7	Ⓐ	Ⓑ	Ⓒ	Ⓓ
8	Ⓐ	Ⓑ	Ⓒ	Ⓓ
9	Ⓐ	Ⓑ	Ⓒ	Ⓓ
10	Ⓐ	Ⓑ	Ⓒ	Ⓓ

DIRECTIONS: Read the website information to answer the next 5 questions. Use the Answer Sheet on page 116.

Legal Aid

Search for [   ] Go

About us   Feedback   News   Other states   Help   Program directory

Are you worried about consulting a lawyer because of the cost? Are you unsure about how to get a good attorney? Don't let these concerns stop you from getting good legal advice when you need it. Your local American Bar Association can provide a list of attorneys. In most cities, people with a low income can get legal services for little or no cost through a legal aid service.

Click on a topic below to find information, sample forms, and facts sheets.

- Abuse
- Children's issues
- Criminal law
- Disability
- Domestic violence
- Health
- Housing
- Immigration
- Taxes
- Work and unemployment

6. Where can some people get legal assistance for free?

A. American Bar Association
B. legal aid service
C. through the telephone directory
D. through a program directory

7. According to the information, why do people not get legal help?

A. They don't think they need it.
B. They are immigrants.
C. They think it will cost too much.
D. They are afraid.

8. Who can get legal assistance for little or no cost?

A. anyone
B. immigrants
C. lawyers
D. people with little money

9. Which of the following is <u>not</u> a topic on the website?

A. personal injury
B. work and unemployment
C. housing
D. domestic violence

10. What can the Bar Association help you with?

A. saving money
B. finding an attorney
C. talking to legal aid
D. using a website

HOW DID YOU DO? Count the number of correct answers on your answer sheet. Record this number in the bar graph on the inside back cover.

Spotlight: Reading

A Read the following sentences. Write the causes and effects on the lines.

1. He had to go to court because he got three traffic tickets.

   Cause: _____

   Effect: _____

2. The Republicans lost seats in the election. As a result, the Democrats took control of the Senate.

   Cause: _____

   Effect: _____

3. Due to the rise in gas prices, bus ridership increased dramatically.

   Cause: _____

   Effect: _____

4. Because of the dramatic decrease in the murder rate, the county saved $20,000 in the cost of prosecution last year.

   Cause: _____

   Effect: _____

5. The people in my neighborhood organized a community watch program. Consequently, crime in our neighborhood has gone down.

   Cause: _____

   Effect: _____

B Combine the following sentences. Use one of the words or phrases in the box to show the cause/effect relationship.

because	since	if
as a result	for this reason	consequently

1. I watch the news every night. I'm very well informed.

   _____

2. The defendant was sentenced to five years in prison. He was found guilty.

   _____

3. She missed three days of work. She got a terrible flu.

   _____

C Read the information and find 3 cause/effect relationships. Write them in the chart below.

Franklin Delano Roosevelt was the 32nd president of the United States. He was also the only president to be elected four times, serving from 1933 until his death on April 12, 1945. When he was 39, Roosevelt contracted polio and had difficulty walking for the rest of his life.

At the time he was elected, the United States was in a terrible economic depression. Roosevelt quickly proposed a sweeping program, the New Deal, that would help businesses economically and provide relief to thousands of unemployed people. It also set up social safety nets, such as Social Security, that are still in effect today.

When the Japanese attacked Pearl Harbor, the United States entered into World War II. Roosevelt led the country through most of the war, dying just before the war ended. He is remembered for his leadership during the devastating depression and war.

Cause	Effect
1.	
2.	
3.	

D Paraphrase the article.

_____

_____

_____

_____

_____

E Answer the questions in complete sentences.

1. Why did Roosevelt have to use a wheelchair?

_____

2. Why did he introduce the policies and programs of the New Deal?

_____

3. Why do you think Roosevelt is one of the most well-known American presidents?

_____

Spotlight: Writing

A Use the diagrams to organize your answers to the cause/effect questions below. Then write a paragraph to answer each question.

1. What are 3 causes of homelessness? Complete the cause/effect diagram.

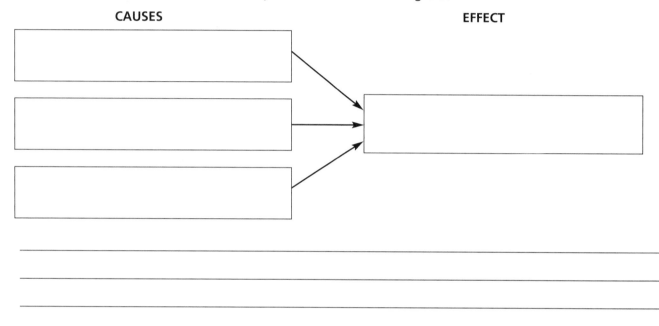

CAUSES   EFFECT

_____

_____

_____

_____

2. What are some effects of violent crime on a community? Complete the cause/effect diagram.

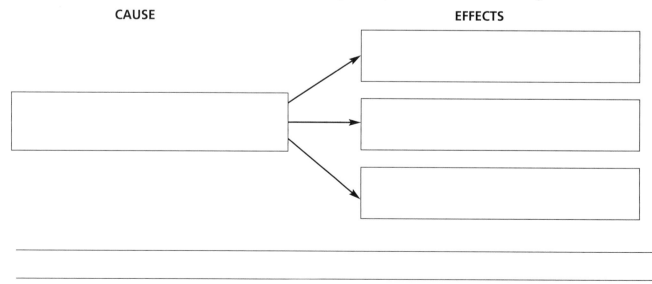

CAUSE   EFFECTS

_____

_____

_____

_____

3. How is the attitude toward domestic violence in the United States similar to the attitude toward it in another country you know? How is it different? Complete the Venn Diagram.

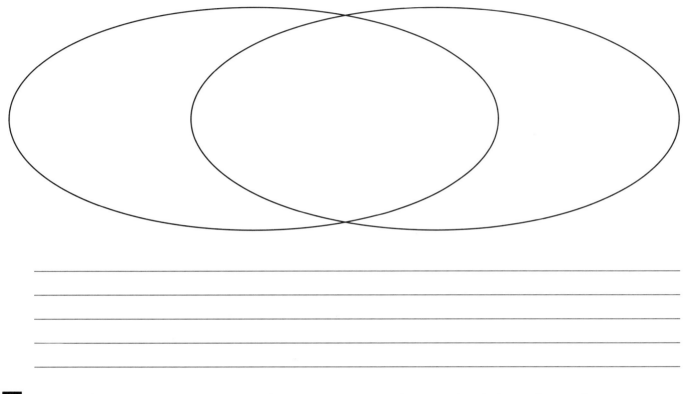

_____

_____

_____

_____

_____

_____

B Create a diagram to organize your ideas in response to the question below. Then write a paragraph.

1. How can someone become a citizen of the United States?

_____

_____

_____

_____

Who's in charge?

A Look at the photos below. Identify a rule the employees are breaking.

John and David

Scott and Lenny

Sara, Meg, and Elise

Work Rules

The following are not permitted:

1. fighting
2. being absent without an excuse
3. violating safety rules
4. wearing inappropriate clothing
5. ignoring work duties
6. failing to observe time limits for breaks
7. using office equipment improperly

---

1. John and David are _____.

2. Scott and Lenny are _____.

3. Sara, Meg, and Elise are _____.

B Look at the photos on page 122 again. Read the situations and suggest answers to the questions.

1. Cindy is the owner of a magazine where John and David work. She comes in to the office with a client and finds John and David playing football. What should she do?

   _____

   _____

2. Scott and Lenny both want to be chosen to work on a team their boss is putting together. The boss finds them fighting in the hall. What should the boss say to them?

   _____

   _____

3. Sara, Meg, and Elise are working on a project together and the deadline is in 2 days. Sara and Elise are looking at something inappropriate on the computer. What should Meg do?

   _____

   _____

C Add a prefix (*dis, il, im, in, un*) to the following words to change the meaning from positive to negative.

_____ legal   _____ literate   _____ legible

_____ proper   _____ possible   _____ mature

_____ appropriate   _____ correct   _____ capable

_____ necessary   _____ acceptable   _____ usual

_____ orderly   _____ connect   _____ agree

D Complete the questions with words from Activity C. Answers can vary.

1. What do you consider _____ behavior at work?

2. Where is it _____ to wear pajamas?

3. How does your teacher react when you give an _____ answer?

4. What kinds of discrimination are _____ in the workplace according to the Equal Employment Opportunity Commission?

5. What should you do if you _____ with something your supervisor asks you to do?

E Answer the questions in Activity D.

1. _____

2. _____

3. _____

4. _____

5. _____

Experience is preferred.

LESSON 2

A Choose the correct form of the words to complete the questions. Then answer the questions.

NOUN	VERB	ADJECTIVE
1. assistant, assistance	assist	XXXXX
2. courtesy	XXXXX	courteous
3. discipline	discipline	disciplinary
4. ignorance	ignore	ignorant
5. possession	possess	possessive
6. preference	prefer	preferable
7. preparation	prepare	preparatory
8. provision, provider	provide	providential, provident
9. recruitment, recruiter	recruit	XXXXX
10. resolution	resolve	resolute

1. What kind of _____ can you give your classmates?

   _____

2. Why should salespeople be _____ to customers?

   _____

3. What _____ action do you think an employee should face if he or she is drunk at work?

   _____

4. What should a supervisor do if employees _____ safety rules?

   _____

5. What interpersonal skills do you think a manager should _____?

   _____

6. What type of job would you_____?

   _____

7. What kind of _____ would you need for your ideal job?

   _____

8. Why should an employer _____ benefits?

   _____

9. How should employers _____ qualified applicants?

   _____

10. If you had a problem with a coworker, how would you _____ it?

   _____

B Read the job responsibilities and complete the Venn Diagram below.

Administrative Assistant	Chief Clerk
• Maintains administrative and personnel files • Maintains systems, procedures, and methods for record keeping • Prepares financial reports and budgets • Interacts with vendors, member agencies, and the public to answer questions and to resolve account and billing discrepancies • Writes reports • Handles questions and concerns of employees, officials, and businesses • Assists supervisor as needed • May supervise volunteers and other support personnel	• Prepares special reports and tabulations according to general directions • Edits reports for completeness and accuracy • Maintains personnel records • Keeps records of leave and nontaxable wages • May prepare and distribute pay checks • Compiles information and records to prepare purchase orders • May compare prices and specifications • Maintains cost records on equipment • Assists supervisor as needed

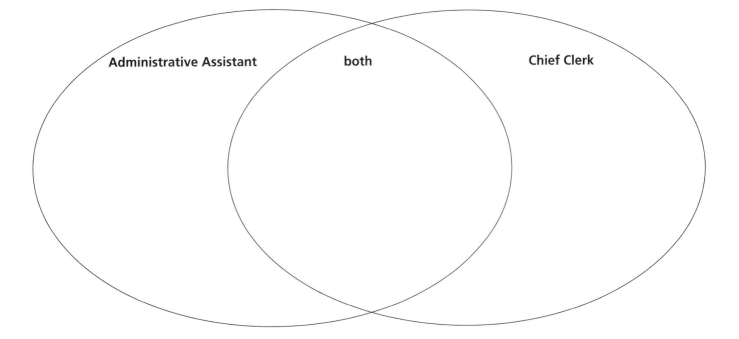

Administrative Assistant   both   Chief Clerk

C Answer the questions.

1. Which job above do you think has more responsibility? Why?

_____

_____

2. Which job above do you think requires more math? Why?

_____

_____

LESSON 3

He spoke very clearly.

A Match the questions and the expanded answers. Write the letters on the lines.

1. Did you enjoy working there? _____
2. Where did you work before that? _____
3. Do you have any supervisory experience? _____
4. How long have you lived in the area? _____
5. Can you design websites? _____
6. What did you study in school? _____
7. Have you worked in a real estate office before? _____

a. Business. I graduated from the university in Monterrey.
b. Yes, actually. I worked for my uncle's company one summer and had to design one there.
c. In a clothing store. I was there for a year and a half.
d. Very much. The people were friendly, and the manager gave me a lot of responsibility.
e. No. But I did work in an apartment management office.
f. About two years. I moved here from New York.
g. Yes, I do. I was a shift supervisor at the clothing store.

B Complete the conversations. Expand on your answer.

1. A: Do you like living here?

   B: _____

2. A: Would you like a job working with customers?

   B: _____

3. A: Would you rather work with other people or have more independence?

   B: _____

4. A: What kind of a position are you looking for?

   B: _____

C Read the interview and answer the questions below.

Interviewer:	I see that you have worked in retail before.
Applicant:	Yeah.
Interviewer:	Could you tell me a little bit about that job?
Applicant:	It was okay. I got to wear what I wanted, and the people were cool.
Interviewer:	What did you do exactly?
Applicant:	Well, I started as, like, a cashier, but after about a year, I got a promotion.
Interviewer:	A promotion?
Applicant:	The manager made me the supervisor of my area. I was responsible for the displays, and trained the new people.
Interviewer:	Did you like the added responsibility?
Applicant:	You know, I really did. I really like designing stuff, so I enjoyed putting the displays together. And I found out that I like teaching people.
Interviewer:	Well, here we appreciate creativity, but we do have a dress code. Our salespeople would not be allowed to wear an outfit like the one you are wearing now. It's too unconventional.
Applicant:	I've noticed that. But I think if you had your salespeople wear some of the more interesting clothes you carry, you would sell more. Some customers might be afraid to try something off the hanger, but if they see it looks good, they might just try it.

1. How would you describe the applicant's language? ☐ businesslike ☐ casual

2. How was the applicant dressed? ☐ in business attire ☐ casually

3. What is one strength of the applicant? ☐ She's responsible. ☐ She's professional.

4. What is one weakness of the applicant? ☐ She's too informal. ☐ She has a negative attitude.

5. Which description of the applicant is most accurate? ☐ She's friendly. ☐ She's polite.

6. Why would she be good working in a clothing store? ☐ She's well-dressed. ☐ She has good, creative ideas.

7. Would you hire the applicant? Why or why not? _____

_____

Performance Evaluations

LESSON 4

A Circle the letter for the behavior that best demonstrates the characteristic.

1. She's very **reliable**.
   A. She always has great ideas.
   B. She completes every assignment on time.
   C. She asks for input from coworkers.
   D. She is very courteous on the phone.

2. He gets high ratings for **creativity**.
   A. He has ideas for new ways to do things.
   B. He gets along well with supervisors.
   C. He is always on time.
   D. He signs up for training.

3. She's fairly **independent**.
   A. She will do any task she's asked to do.
   B. She often requires assistance.
   C. She can work without supervision.
   D. She has her own opinions.

4. He has difficulty exercising **initiative**.
   A. He needs clearly defined tasks.
   B. He's often late.
   C. He volunteers for projects.
   D. He often argues with coworkers.

5. His **interpersonal skills** are his greatest strength.
   A. He doesn't require supervision.
   B. He is prompt for meetings.
   C. He has expanded his skills.
   D. He listens well, and asks for input.

B Read the following notes and fill out the evaluation form with complete sentences. Rate the employee based on the comments.

Ben Okomo: Late almost every day, customers and coworkers like him a lot, very polite and helpful, follows directions well, but needs to be supervised on new tasks. Does not contribute new ideas, but very good at selling and displaying shoes. Knows a lot about the merchandise. Does not make mistakes. Good team player.

Employee Performance Evaluation	EMPLOYEE *Ben Okomo*	TITLE *Store Associate*
	DEPARTMENT *Men's Shoes*	EMPLOYEE NO. *351*

TYPE OF EVALUATION

☑ ANNUAL ☐ PROMOTION ☐ MERIT ☐ OTHER

DIRECTIONS: Evaluate the employee's work performance as it relates to the requirements of the job. Write the number that best describes the employee's performance since the last evaluation.

1 = Excellent   **2** = Very Good   **3** = Satisfactory   **4** = Needs Improvement   **5** = Unsatisfactory

Job Responsibilities	Rating	Comments
DEPENDABILITY The employee is on time and follows the rules for breaks and attendance.		
BEHAVIOR The employee is polite on the job.		
CREATIVITY The employee suggests ideas and better ways of accomplishing goals.		
RELIABILITY The employee can be relied on to efficiently complete a job.		
INDEPENDENCE The employee accomplishes work with little or no supervision.		
INITIATIVE The employee looks for new tasks and expands abilities professionally.		
INTERPERSONAL SKILLS The employee is willing and able to communicate, cooperate, and work with coworkers, supervisors, and customers.		
JOB SKILLS The employee has the appropriate skills to do the job well.		

5
LESSON

If I had known, . . .

A Complete the sentences with the past perfect.

1. We _____ (just/start) the meeting when the fire alarm went off.

2. The store _____ (already/close) when I got there.

3. Someone broke in because the manager _____ (forget) to lock the door.

4. He _____ (just/receive) a good evaluation, so he was in a good mood.

5. They _____ (finally/reach) an agreement when they got the phone call.

6. When I got the message, I _____ (already/delete) the file.

7. She was fired when the boss found out she _____ (leave) the office unattended.

B Read the timeline. Complete the paragraph using an appropriate tense for the verb in parentheses.

	wins Mr. Universe, 1970	becomes naturalized citizen, 1983	marries Maria Shriver, 1986	elected Governor of California, 2003
	moves to the United States, 1968	in movie "Pumping Iron" 1977	becomes Chairman of the President's Council on Physical Fitness and Sports, 1990–1993	

born in Graz, 1947   in movie "Conan the Barbarian" 1982   in movie "Terminator" 1984

Arnold Schwarzenegger _____ (1) born in Graz, Austria in 1947. He _____ (2) to the United States at the age of 21. He first _____ (3) famous with the movie "Pumping Iron." By then, Schwarzenegger _____ (4) Mr. Universe, as well as several other body-building titles. When he _____ (5) the highly successful movie "Terminator" in 1984, he _____ (6) his American citizenship. By the time he _____ (7) Maria Shriver, Schwarzenegger _____ (8) in several action movies, but he later _____ (9) in comedies as well. President George H.W. Bush _____ (10) Schwarzenegger to be Chairman of the President's Council on Physical Fitness. On November 17, 2003, Arnold Schwarzenegger _____ (11) Governor of California.

(1) be
(2) move
(3) become
(4) win
(5) make
(6) recently/get
(7) marry
(8) already/star
(9) act
(10) appoint
(11) elect

C Complete the sentences with the correct form of the verb in parentheses.

1. They would have hired me if I _____ (have) a degree.

2. If she had listened to my advice, she _____ (not/marry) him.

3. If it _____ (not/rain), we wouldn't have missed the bus.

4. The company would have closed if we _____ (not/lay off) all those people.

5. If only Jack _____ (arrive) in time, he would have won the vacation.

6. If you _____ (not/move) here, we wouldn't have met.

7. If Maria had taken the message correctly, I _____ (call) you back.

8. I wouldn't have missed my connection if my first flight _____ (leave) on time.

9. They would have understood the policy if they _____ (come) to the meeting.

10. I think we _____ (finish) more quickly if you _____ (be) here.

11. If more people _____ (vote), Lily would have been elected.

12. If I _____ (think) of it, I would have emailed everyone.

13. If we _____ (get) the contract, we _____ (earn) millions.

14. If she _____ (not/make) that mistake, she _____ (win) the competition.

D Complete the note with the correct form of the verbs in parentheses.

Tony,

I _____ (1. leave) for the airport now.
Susan _____ (2. arrive) at 10 P.M. She
_____ (3. not/tell) me until this afternoon. If
I _____ (4. know), I _____
(5. clean) the apartment. Sorry to ask you this, but can you
tidy things up a bit? It _____ (6. look) like a
hurricane hit. I _____ (7. not/want) her to
think we _____ (8. be) slobs—even if we
_____ (9. be). By the way, when I
_____ (10. get) home today, your mom
_____ (11. already/call) _five_ times. You really
should call her.

Thanks, Hugh

WORK

LESSON

What's happening to the U.S. workforce?

A Study the charts and read the sentences below. Check (✓) *True* or *False*.

	True	False
1. These charts show what might happen in the workforce in the future.	☐	☐
2. These charts give information about the workforce for the next twenty years.	☐	☐
3. Chart 1 says that by 2012 there might be a need for about 600,000 more registered nurses in the workforce.	☐	☐
4. According to Chart 2, there will be about 25,000 fewer positions for farmers and ranchers in the U.S. workforce by 2012.	☐	☐
5. According to Chart 2, the need for farmers and ranchers will decrease more than the need for sewing machine operators.	☐	☐

Chart 1:

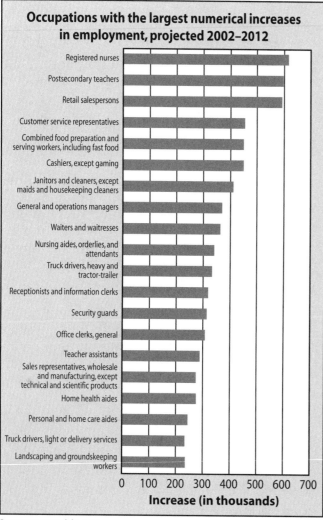

Occupations with the largest numerical increases in employment, projected 2002–2012

Chart 2:

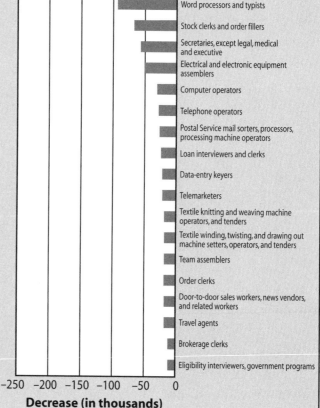

Job declines in occupations with the largest numerical decreases in employment, projected 2002–2012

Source: www.bls.gov

B Use the charts on page 132 to answer the questions below. Circle your answers.

1. Which of these occupations will probably employ more people in the future than today?
   A. travel agents   B. home health aides   C. telemarketers

2. Which of these occupations will probably employ fewer people in the future than today?
   A. security guards   B. cashiers   C. computer operators

3. The number of employees in which of these jobs will probably increase the most?
   A. retail salespeople   B. office clerks   C. waiters

4. The number of employees in which of these jobs will probably decrease the most?
   A. textile operators   B. order clerks   C. telephone operators

C What advice would you give to each of these people?

1. Anita, a high school student, is interested in both computers and nursing. What career planning advice could you give her? Why?

   Your advice:

2. Pépé would like to have a job working with people. He's especially interested in working in sales. What career planning advice could you give him? Why?

   Your advice:

 TAKE IT ONLINE: Use your favorite search engine to find the U.S. Department of Labor, Bureau of Labor Statistics. On the Bureau of Labor Statistics website, find a chart with information that is interesting to you. List 3 interesting things you learned from the chart.

   1. _____

   2. _____

   3. _____

133

COMMUNITY

LESSON

Keep on learning.

A Read the questions in the chart below and predict the answers. Then read the information below the chart and look for the answers to the questions.

Questions	My answers before reading the text	My answers after reading the text
1) What is a "lifelong learner"?		
2) What is a GED certificate?		
3) Where can you get information about GED classes in your area?		
4) What is the most common reason for taking adult education courses?		

Adult Education

Learning does not have to end when you become an adult. In the U.S., people are encouraged to become "lifelong learners." If you are 16 years of age or older and have not finished high school, you can take Adult Secondary Education (ASE) classes. These classes prepare you to earn a General Educational Development (GED) certificate. Most U.S. employers consider a GED certificate to be equal to a regular high school diploma. In many areas, GED preparation classes are free or low-cost. Look in the phone book under "Adult Education" or call your local school district office for information.

Many adults take classes to learn more about a subject that interests them or to learn new skills that can help them in their jobs. Many public school systems and local community colleges offer classes in a wide range of subjects for adults. Anyone can enroll in these classes which generally have low fees. Check with your local school system or community college to find out what classes are available, how much they cost, and how to enroll.

Participation rates in adult education activities in 2001

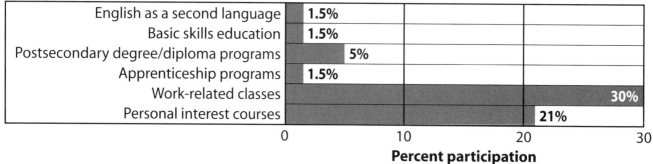

English as a second language	1.5%		
Basic skills education	1.5%		
Postsecondary degree/diploma programs	5%		
Apprenticeship programs	1.5%		
Work-related classes			30%
Personal interest courses		21%	

0   10   20   30

Percent participation

Source: U.S. Department of Education, National Center for Education Statistics

B Study the ad from a telephone book. Then read the statements below and check (✓) *True* or *False*.

FcTc *Franklin Community Technical College*

Over 40 liberal arts and career programs to choose from!

Careers in Demand . . .
Building Construction
Commercial Design
HVAC & Refrigeration
Liberal Arts
Nursing

Associate Degrees, Certificates
Non-Credit Courses
Full Time, Part Time
Days, Evenings
Weekends and On-line
Financial Aid Available

555-9339

		True	False
1.	You can take classes in the evening at Franklin Community Technical College.	☐	☐
2.	This school offers liberal arts courses only.	☐	☐
3.	You can take courses from your home using your computer.	☐	☐
4.	This school helps some students pay for their courses.	☐	☐
5.	You can only take courses here if you want to get a degree.	☐	☐
6.	You can get training for a job at this school	☐	☐

★ ★

TAKE IT OUTSIDE: Interview 3 friends or neighbors. Ask them where they last went to school, what they studied, and what they liked and disliked about the school. Write what you learned in the chart below.

Name of school	Area of study	Likes and dislikes
1)		
2)		
3)		

★ ★

TAKE IT ONLINE: Using your favorite search engine, type in the name of your town or a town nearby. When you get to the town's website, look for information about adult education programs. On the lines below, list 3 things you learned.

1. _____

2. _____

3. _____

REVIEW

LESSON

Practice Test

DIRECTIONS: Read the job descriptions to answer the next 5 questions. Use the Answer Sheet on page 137.

ADMINISTRATIVE ASSISTANT

Responsibilities:

- Assist department chair
- Update classes in mainframe computer
- Maintain student records
- Submit end-of-term forms, including grades and attendance records
- Assist instructors with forms

Skills:

Can use office software; previous experience in office setting

Salary: $12 an hour

FINANCIAL AID COUNSELOR

Responsibilities:

- Meet with and counsel students on financial aid process
- Review financial aid applications
- Maintain student financial aid records in mainframe computer
- Oversee work-study positions as needed

Skills:

B.A. required in business, education, or counseling; 2 years experience in higher ed. setting

Salary: $30,000 annually

CASHIER

Responsibilities:

- Handle tuition payments, including cash, check, or credit payments
- Maintain records
- Handle customer questions and concerns
- Count and balance money, prepare deposits

Skills:

1 year experience as cashier

Salary: $10 an hour

REGISTRAR

Responsibilities:

- Maintain student registration records
- Use computer registration system
- Handle student questions, concerns, complaints
- Provide excellent service

Skills:

B.A. in administration required, M.A. preferred, plus 3 years experience in educational setting

Salary: $35,000+

1. Which job is the highest paying?

   A. Administrative assistant

   B. Cashier

   C. Financial aid counselor

   D. Registrar

2. Which job has the lowest salary?

   A. Administrative assistant

   B. Cashier

   C. Financial aid counselor

   D. Registrar

3. Which job does not require computer use?

   A. Administrative assistant

   B. Cashier

   C. Financial aid counselor

   D. Registrar

4. Which job requires the most experience?

   A. Administrative assistant

   B. Cashier

   C. Financial aid counselor

   D. Registrar

5. Which job asks for the most education?

   A. Administrative assistant

   B. Cashier

   C. Financial aid counselor

   D. Registrar

DIRECTIONS: Read the article to answer the next 5 questions. Use the Answer Sheet.

How to Get That Job

Your job hunt is a process that can take a long time. Once you have decided on a career and have focused on particular employers, you should prepare for the interview.

- Research the potential employer. You can talk to people in the field, go online, or go to the library to find out as much as possible about the organization. This kind of research will help you ask good questions, and will show that you are well informed. You can also learn if the employer offers good benefits.
- Present yourself in the best possible way. Dress neatly and in a professional manner. Arrive a few minutes before the interview. Be friendly and polite to everyone you meet, including the receptionist.
- Be positive in the interview. Focus on your strengths and how you are addressing any possible weaknesses. Be honest.
- Bring the names and contact information of possible references with you in case you are asked for references.

ANSWER SHEET

1	Ⓐ	Ⓑ	Ⓒ	Ⓓ
2	Ⓐ	Ⓑ	Ⓒ	Ⓓ
3	Ⓐ	Ⓑ	Ⓒ	Ⓓ
4	Ⓐ	Ⓑ	Ⓒ	Ⓓ
5	Ⓐ	Ⓑ	Ⓒ	Ⓓ
6	Ⓐ	Ⓑ	Ⓒ	Ⓓ
7	Ⓐ	Ⓑ	Ⓒ	Ⓓ
8	Ⓐ	Ⓑ	Ⓒ	Ⓓ
9	Ⓐ	Ⓑ	Ⓒ	Ⓓ
10	Ⓐ	Ⓑ	Ⓒ	Ⓓ

6. What is one way to prepare good questions to ask an interviewer?

A. arrive early
B. do research online
C. focus on your strengths
D. learn if they offer good benefits

7. Who should you be friendly to?

A. the interviewer
B. the supervisor
C. the receptionist
D. everyone

8. What should you bring with you?

A. names of people who know you
B. names and contact information for references
C. information on benefits
D. an application form

9. Which is **not** true?

A. You should talk mostly about your strengths, not your weaknesses.
B. You should be honest about areas you are not strong in.
C. You should dress neatly.
D. You shouldn't ask questions.

10. What should you do first?

A. choose a career
B. research employers
C. dress well
D. arrive a little early

HOW DID YOU DO? Count the number of correct answers on your answer sheet. Record this number in the bar graph on the inside back cover.

Spotlight: Reading

A Complete the sentences with the correct word or phrase to indicate the sequence of events.

first	finally	today	then	after	before
during	while	meanwhile	when	after that	

_____ I decided to make a special dessert, nut meringue pie.

_____ my childhood, my mother always made it for me on my birthday.

So I called her and got the recipe. _____ things started to go wrong.

_____, I drove to the store and had a flat tire. _____

I fixed the flat and went to the store, I found out I didn't have my checkbook. _____

I could pay for the ingredients, I had to go all the way back home. _____,

it had started snowing and the streets were slippery. _____ I hit the

brakes suddenly, the eggs flew out of the carton. _____ I had to stop and

clean up the eggs. Of course, I had to go back to the store for more eggs. _____,

I made it home with the ingredients, only to find the electricity was out!

B Create a timeline for the story in Activity A.

C Read this story by Aesop and underline the words that help you follow the sequence of events.

The Lion and the Mouse

ONCE when a Lion was asleep a little Mouse began running up and down upon him; this soon wakened the Lion, who placed his huge paw upon him, and opened his big jaws to swallow him. "Pardon, O King," cried the little Mouse: "forgive me this time, I shall never forget it: who knows but what I may be able to do you a turn some of these days?" The Lion was so tickled at the idea of the Mouse being able to help him, that he lifted up his paw and let him go. Some time after the Lion was caught in a trap, and the hunters, who desired to carry him alive to the King, tied him to a tree while they went in search of a wagon to carry him on. Just then the little

Mouse happened to pass by, and seeing the sad plight in which the Lion was, went up to him and soon gnawed away the ropes that bound the King of the Beasts. "Was I not right?" said the little Mouse.

"Little friends may prove great friends."

D Rewrite the story in your own words.

_____

_____

_____

_____

_____

_____

_____

_____

_____

Spotlight: Writing

A Number the activities to indicate the sequence of events in the writing process.

_____ Exchange drafts with someone to get and give feedback.

_____ Talk to one or more people about your ideas.

_____ Write a first draft.

_____ Organize your ideas through a mind-map or outline.

_____ Revise the draft to incorporate feedback and new ideas.

_____ Generate initial ideas through quick-writing.

B Read this student's draft and answer the questions below.

> After we spend the whole night sleeping usually in the morning we ate breakfast. Some people has time and make their breakfast at home. However, other people find it easier to get their food at a fast food restaurant. This is a place where people can get their food fast in a comfortable place. People can also read a newspaper while they are eating. Other people can has a conversation until they decide to leave. Also people may enjoy her coffee. You can see many different people entering and leaving this restaurant.

1. What is the topic?

_____

2. What details does the writer include?

_____

_____

3. What do you think the writer should add to this essay?

_____

_____

4. Is there anything unclear or unnecessary? If so, what?

_____

_____

5. Find and circle 4 grammatical mistakes in the draft. Then correct the mistakes.

_____

_____

C Draft an essay about a favorite place. Follow the steps.

1. Quickwrite about a favorite place in the space below.

2. Map your ideas.

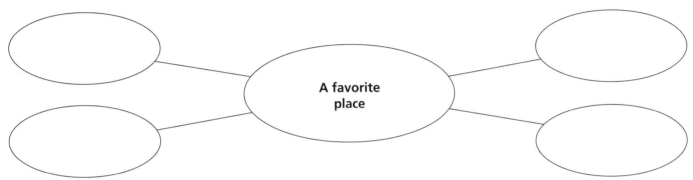

A favorite place

3. Write a first draft.

LESSON 1

It's not in the budget.

A Look at the items Sandy bought yesterday. Write the amounts in the appropriate places on her monthly expense record below.

$45.00

$3.79

$2.50

$8.50

$6.75

TRANSPORT.	FOOD	ENTERTAIN.	MISC.	CLOTHING
5/1 bus pass $40.00	5/3 groceries $275.00	5/10 concert $32.00	5/5 books $33.80	5/6 skirt $38.00
5/16 parking $6.00	5/12 lunch $11.50	5/12 video $4.25	5/11 shampoo $3.00	5/6 T-shirt $15.00
5/24 taxi $7.30	5/22 groceries $25.00	5/26 video $4.25	5/16 cards $5.75	5/20 jacket $59.00
5/27	5/27	5/27	5/27	5/27
Total =	Total =	Total =	Total =	Total =

B Answer the questions about Sandy's purchases and budget.

1. Sandy budgeted $50 for entertainment this month. Is her actual spending over or under budget now? _____

2. She has a monthly spending goal of $200 or less on clothes. What will she have to do to meet this goal? _____

3. If Sandy wanted to reduce her spending, what do you think she could have done without? _____

4. Approximately what percentage of Sandy's total expenses so far this month has been spent on food? _____

C Classify the following expenses into fixed (the same every month) or variable (can change every month) expenses.

mortgage payment	school loan payments	groceries	car payments
gas	utilities	child care	clothing
health insurance	rent	entertainment	bus pass

FIXED	VARIABLE

D Complete the chart with the correct form of the words. Then complete the questions below and answer them.

NOUN	VERB	ADJECTIVE
1.	entertain	entertaining
2.	utilize	XXXXX
3.	transport	transportable
4. miscellany	XXXXX	
5.	clothe	XXXXX
6.	invest	XXXXX
7. action	act	

1. How much did you spend on _____ last month?

_____

2. Are your _____ higher or lower in the summer?

_____

3. What form of _____ do you usually take to school?

_____

4. What _____ expenses did you have last week?

_____

5. Who spends the most on _____ in your household?

_____

6. What kind of _____ do you have?

_____

7. Is your _____ spending usually higher or lower than your spending goals?

_____

2
LESSON

Do you have an IRA?

A Complete the sentences with a word or phrase from the box.

certificate of deposit	deficit	penalty	fixed	maxed out
perks	set back	shares	specific	stock

1. The interest rate on a _____ is higher than on a regular savings account.

2. That new car _____ me _____ a few thousand dollars.

3. Although adjustable rate mortgages are cheaper right now, in the long run a _____ rate mortgage might save you more money and it's predictable.

4. There's a _____ for bouncing checks.

5. I couldn't buy the video game. I _____ my credit card.

6. Downtown Bank is offering _____ to customers who open accounts this month.

7. His grandparents left him _____ of _____ in a Fortune 500 company.

B Unscramble the words to write questions about money.

1. if / don't / what / you / pay / happens / your credit card bill / on time

   _____

2. some differences / are / between / credit cards / what

   _____

3. of / some advantages / what / a CD / are

   _____

4. invest / why / in an IRA / you / should

   _____

5. governments / have / when / a deficit / do

   _____

C Answer the questions in Activity B.

1. _____

2. _____

3. _____

4. _____

5. _____

D Look at the graph to answer the questions below.

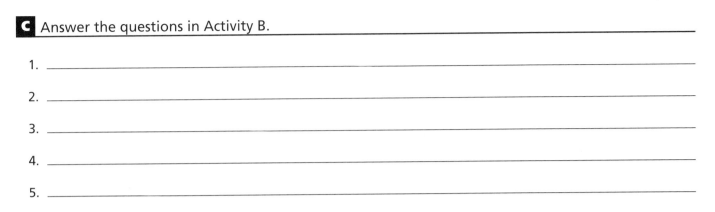

Assets and Debts for people with incomes between $625,000 and $1 million (1998)

1. For wealthy Americans with incomes between $625,000 and $1 million, who has greater debt (including mortgages), men or women? _____

2. Who has more wealth invested in personal homes? _____

3. Where do wealthy men invest the least? _____

4. Where do wealthy women invest the most? _____

5. Who has more wealth invested in homes that are not for personal use? _____

6. In which asset category are men and women almost equal? _____

E Rate the investments from 1 to 5, with 1 being the best.

_____ your personal residence

_____ stock

_____ cash, bank accounts, money markets

_____ retirement accounts (not social security)

_____ other (_____)

145

3 LESSON

Does this account earn interest?

A Number each conversation in order starting with #1.

Conversation A: BankPlus

_____ Well, do you just have one type of checking account?

_____ What are the differences?

___1___ Hi. How can I help you?

_____ Whoa. What about the free checking account?

_____ Hi. I wanted to ask a few questions about opening a checking account.

_____ Well, you don't earn interest, but there is no minimum balance and no monthly service fee.

_____ I think I'll try that one.

_____ No, BankPlus actually offers two types of accounts, free checking and deluxe checking.

_____ With deluxe checking you get free checks, and can earn interest, but you must have a minimum balance of $2,500 in your account.

_____ Sure. What would you like to know?

Conversation B: Grand Bank

_____ The Premium account requires a minimum balance of $1,500. With the Gold Star account, you need to maintain a minimum balance of $5,000, but you earn interest.

_____ Sure. I'd be happy to answer your questions. What would you like to know?

_____ Does Grand Bank offer free checks with checking accounts?

_____ Is there a minimum balance on basic checking?

_____ Yes, we do, with our Premium and Gold Star accounts. With basic checking the first 500 checks are free, but there is a charge for additional checks.

_____ No. And there is no monthly service fee either. The other two charge fees when you drop below the minimums.

___1___ Excuse me. I'd like some information about checking accounts.

_____ I think I'd like to open a Premium account.

_____ What are some other differences?

B Read the sentences and circle *True* or *False*.

1. The Gold Star account requires a higher minimum balance than BankPlus' deluxe checking account.   TRUE   FALSE

2. BankPlus does not offer interest on its checking accounts.   TRUE   FALSE

3. BankPlus offers more types of checking accounts than Grand Bank.   TRUE   FALSE

4. Both banks offer free checks with all accounts.   TRUE   FALSE

5. Grand Bank has a greater range of options than BankPlus.   TRUE   FALSE

C Complete the Venn Diagram to compare the two banks in Activity A.

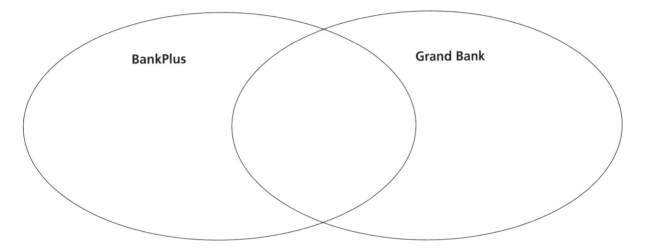

BankPlus   Grand Bank

D Complete the conversations. Confirm the information.

1. A: You need a minimum deposit of $50 to open a savings account.

   B: _____

   A: Yes, that's right, fifty.

2. A: If you want overdraft protection, you can link your checking account to a savings or money market account.

   B: _____

   A: Yes. Linking to another account allows the bank to move funds to cover your overdraft.

3. A: If you link it to a savings account and there is an overdraft, your overdrawn checking account will be charged $5.

   B: _____

   A: That's right. The $5 will come out of the checking account.

4. A: For a fixed-rate CD, you need a minimum deposit of $2,500.

   B: _____

   A: Yes. The minimum deposit on the fixed rate CD is two thousand five hundred.

4 LESSON

Preventing Consumer Fraud

A Preview the article below and check (✓) the questions you think it will answer.

❑ What are some types of consumer fraud that immigrants may experience?

❑ How can immigrants avoid becoming victims of fraud?

❑ What are the possible punishments someone committing fraud might face?

❑ How are immigrants different from other consumers?

B Read the article and complete the sentences with words from the box.

black market	bogus	credit	crooks	fees
fortunately	guard	security	fraud	

Immigrants and Consumer Fraud

Immigrants may be more likely to become victims of _____ than other consumers because of language problems and unfamiliarity with the American market. Most Americans are aware of the services available to help them and can avoid becoming victims, but many new immigrants don't know basic consumer protection information. _____ can take advantage of immigrants in the following areas.

Credit offers: Newcomers often need to establish _____ so they can buy a car or rent an apartment. Dishonest people may offer to help an immigrant get credit, but they will charge a high fee.

Employment agencies: Some so-called "agencies" provide _____ job listings for a fee. Not only are the job leads false, the companies themselves may not exist.

Private specialized schools: Many for-profit schools design classes to attract the working immigrant. They promise to teach English and other marketable job skills, but such schools may cost a lot and deliver little.

Money wiring: Another way businesses take advantage of immigrants is to offer money transfers for very high _____. Immigrants often send money to families in other countries, and don't always have bank accounts, so they can be victimized by these businesses.

Used car sales: Immigrants often lack the English skills necessary to read and understand contracts. However, they do need cars to get to work. Dishonest used car salespeople can take advantage of this situation by charging higher prices and interest rates.

Immigrants can best _____ against these kinds of fraud by becoming educated. Adult education programs and community agencies should provide information on fraud.

C Answer these questions about the article on page 148.

1. Why do criminals often select immigrants as the targets of fraud?

   _____

2. Why do some immigrants use very high-priced money wiring services?

   _____

3. What are some ways that knowing more English could help immigrants guard against fraud?

   _____

4. What are some types of fraud that immigrants may experience?

   _____

5. How can communities help reduce these kinds of fraud?

   _____

D Choose one of the questions below. Write a paragraph about your experience.

1. Have you or someone you know been the victim of consumer fraud? If so, what happened?

2. What problems have you experienced because you are an immigrant or because of your English skills?

   _____

   _____

   _____

   _____

   _____

   _____

   _____

   _____

   _____

   _____

   _____

   _____

LESSON 5

She said it was a good deal.

A Add appropriate punctuation to the conversation below. Follow the examples.

EXAMPLES: *Mary said I finished my homework* ⟶ *Mary said, "I finished my homework."*

You are late the supervisor said ⟶ *"You are late," the supervisor said.*

1. I sure got in a lot of trouble at work said Ming My boss was mad because I was late

2. That's too bad said Paul

3. Ming said Now I'm worried about taking the day off on Friday

4. Paul said We should postpone our trip to the beach

5. That's a good idea agreed Ming

6. Maybe we can go in a month suggested Paul

7. Okay said Ming I'm going to talk to my boss about it

8. Paul said That's settled then I'll change the reservations

B Rewrite each sentence in Activity A as speech reported soon after. Change the pronouns. You do not have to change the tenses.

1. _____

2. _____

3. _____

4. _____

5. _____

6. _____

7. _____

8. _____

C Rewrite each sentence in Activity B as speech reported much later. Change the tenses.

1. _____

2. _____

3. _____

4. _____

5. _____

6. _____

7. _____

8. _____

D Rewrite the sentences below as reported speech. Change the pronouns and the tenses.

1. "I can't come to the party," said Yolanda.

   _____

2. Rob said, "We're going out later."

   _____

3. Mark said, "I just bought a new car."

   _____

4. "The interest rates on the Gold Star account are higher," said the bank officer.

   _____

5. "You need to protect yourself against fraud," warned the teacher.

   _____

E Answer the questions about yourself.

1. What is the best thing one of your parents ever said to you?

   _____

2. What has someone said to inspire you?

   _____

3. What is something you said that you regret?

   _____

How can you teach children about money?

A Read the story and answer the questions below.

Financial Literacy for Kids: Money Lessons Should Start Young
by Gregory Keer

Growing up in a southeast Los Angeles neighborhood, Alicia Mendiola and her siblings were raised in a household where frugality[1] ruled. Her parents, Mexican immigrants, didn't have much money and knew that living within their means[2] meant a brighter future for their large family.

"My father had pride in having perfect credit and never bought what he could not afford," says Mendiola. "Fast food was a luxury. Everyone took turns getting new shoes, and sometimes your turn never came. After years of living in housing projects, my father bought us a home because he had good credit."

Mendiola learned from her parents' attitude towards money. The single mother struggled[3] to put herself through college and support her daughter, Irene. But today Mendiola is an assistant professor of child development at East Los Angeles College and owns a condominium in Pasadena. Despite the temptation[4] of easy credit[5], Mendiola never got into debt.

Mendiola taught her own daughter the same lesson. Once Irene entered college, Mendiola gave her daughter a fixed amount of money to spend. The budget taught her daughter how to "prioritize her purchases," she says.

---

[1] frugality: being very careful about money
[2] living within their means: not spending more money than they had
[3] struggled: worked very hard
[4] temptation: desire for something
[5] easy credit: money that is easy to borrow

"Financial Literacy for Kids: Money Lessons Should Start Young," by Gregory Keer from *L.A. Parent* at http://losangeles.parenthood.com. Used by permission of the author.

1. What lessons did Alicia's parents teach her about money?

_____

2. How did they teach her these lessons?

_____

3. How were her parents frugal?

_____

4. How do you think Alicia avoided getting into debt while she was in college?

_____

5. What lesson about money did Alicia teach her daughter?

_____

6. How did Alicia teach her daughter this lesson?

_____

B Answer the questions below with information about yourself.

1. What was one thing you learned about money from your parents?

   _____

2. How did your parents teach you this lesson?

   _____

3. What is the most important thing parents should teach their children about money?

   _____

4. How could you teach children to "prioritize their purchases"?

   _____

5. What do you think schools should teach children about money?

   _____

C Match the proverbs with their meanings. Write the letters on the lines.

Proverbs	Meanings
1. A fool and his money are soon parted. _____	a. Money causes a lot of problems.
2. Easy come, easy go. _____	b. If you have money, people listen to you.
3. Money is the root of all evil. _____	c. Your life won't be easy if you marry someone only because he or she is rich.
4. Money talks. _____	d. If you aren't smart with your money, you won't have it for very long.
5. Money doesn't buy happiness. _____	e. It's easy to spend money that you haven't worked hard to earn.
6. If you marry for money, you will earn it. _____	f. It's possible to be rich and unhappy or poor and happy.

★ ★

TAKE IT OUTSIDE: Ask 3 friends or classmates for a proverb about money. Then ask them what the proverb means. Write what you learn in the chart below.

Proverb	Meaning

★ ★

 TAKE IT ONLINE: Use your favorite search engine to look for parenting magazines. Look for 3 articles with ideas for teaching children about money. Write down the titles of the articles and then discuss them with your classmates. Evaluate the titles to determine which article would be most interesting, then read that article.

COMMUNITY LESSON

How much is the government in debt?

A What do you think? Read the statements below and check (✓) *True* or *False* in column 2.

Statements	My answers before reading the article		My answers after reading the article	
	True	False	True	False
1. The U.S. government is in debt now.	☐	☐	☐	☐
2. The U.S. government owes money to other countries.	☐	☐	☐	☐
3. The U.S. government has to pay interest on the national debt.	☐	☐	☐	☐
4. The amount of interest the government pays on the national debt is almost as much as the government pays for defense.	☐	☐	☐	☐
5. The U.S. national debt is the same as the U.S. budget deficit.	☐	☐	☐	☐

B Read the information below to check your answers from Activity A. Then check (✓) the correct answers in column 3 above.

The U.S. National Debt

On February 11, 2005, the National Debt of the United States was $7,629,320,147,691.17. That was the total amount of money that the government owed. It's a lot of money! If each person in the United States had to pay an equal share of the debt, it would cost each of us $25,812.86. So who exactly do we owe all this money to? According to the pie chart below, the largest amount of money is owed to the Federal Reserve Bank and to other government accounts. In other words, it's money we borrowed from ourselves. But it's money either we or future generations have to pay back.

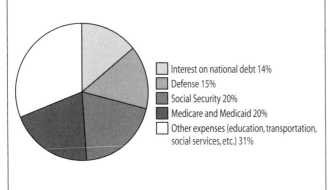

Interest on national debt 14%
Defense 15%
Social Security 20%
Medicare and Medicaid 20%
Other expenses (education, transportation, social services, etc.) 31%

The U.S. Budget Deficit

In 2002 the U.S. government collected about $1.9 trillion in taxes but it spent about $2 trillion. Whenever the government spends more than it collects in a year, it has a budget deficit. And where did the government spend that $2 trillion? Take a look at the chart below to see.

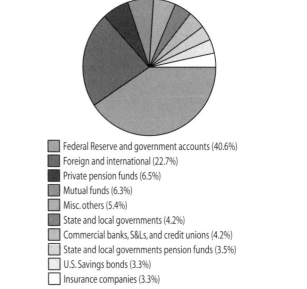

Federal Reserve and government accounts (40.6%)
Foreign and international (22.7%)
Private pension funds (6.5%)
Mutual funds (6.3%)
Misc. others (5.4%)
State and local governments (4.2%)
Commercial banks, S&Ls, and credit unions (4.2%)
State and local governments pension funds (3.5%)
U.S. Savings bonds (3.3%)
Insurance companies (3.3%)

"Who We Owe Money To," U.S. National Debt Clock at www.brillig.com. Images courtesy of Ed Hall.

C Answer these questions.

1. If the government collects $1.9 trillion dollars and spends $2 trillion in one year, does it have a surplus or a deficit? _____

2. Let's say that the government spends $2 trillion in one year. If 10% of its expenses are used to pay interest on the national debt, how much money is that? _____

3. Let's say that your expenses for one year came to $30,000. If 15% of your expenses went to paying interest on your debt, how much money would that be? _____

4. What does the chart below tell you about the U.S. national debt? Write 3 things.

   1) _____

   2) _____

   3) _____

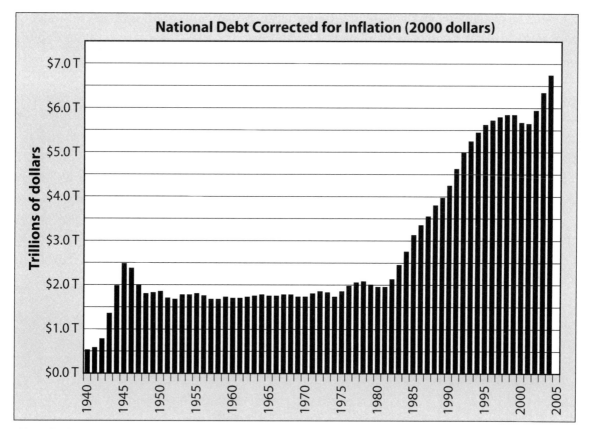

"National Debt Corrected for Inflation (2000 dollars)," U.S. National Debt Clock at www.brillig.com. Image courtesy of Ed Hall.

TAKE IT ONLINE: Use your favorite search engine to look for the U.S. National Debt Clock. Write the current amount of the national debt in the box below.

$ _____

REVIEW
LESSON

Practice Test

DIRECTIONS: Read the article to answer the next 5 questions. Use the Answer Sheet on page 157.

Payment Methods

There are several different ways to pay for products and services, and they each have advantages and disadvantages. Many people are uncomfortable paying for large items with cash because it can be dangerous to carry around a lot of money. However, cash payments are accepted for most purchases and certainly don't involve paying interest.

Many Americans pay for purchases both large and small with credit. When you use credit, you are basically borrowing money at an interest rate to pay for something. People often use credit cards, especially when they are buying something relatively small, such as clothes or groceries. We also say people are using credit when they take out a loan to buy something big, such as a car. Although credit is convenient, it will usually cost more in the long run.

People also write checks to pay for goods and services. This method does not involve paying interest or carrying around large sums of money. Sometimes people pay a small fee to write a check. Usually you need to have a photo ID if you want to write a check.

Another form of payment is the debit card. It is convenient like a credit card, but unlike credit cards, debit cards draw on existing money in an account, rather than on borrowed money.

Still others use money orders to pay for goods and services, especially if they don't have a checking account. Money orders are often used to pay bills because they can be mailed. You usually pay a fee for a money order. You can buy them at post offices, banks, and some stores.

1. How many payment methods are mentioned?
   A. five
   B. two
   C. three
   D. four

2. Which form of payment is basically borrowing money?
   A. cash
   B. money orders
   C. credit
   D. debit

3. What is one problem with using a credit card?
   A. It's not convenient.
   B. It's not accepted everywhere.
   C. It usually means you pay interest.
   D. You can only use it at post offices and banks.

4. Which form of payment can you buy at some stores?
   A. credit card
   B. debit card
   C. check
   D. money order

5. Which form of payment is most like a credit card in terms of convenience?
   A. credit card
   B. debit card
   C. check
   D. money order

DIRECTIONS: Read the graph to answer the next 5 questions. Use the Answer Sheet.

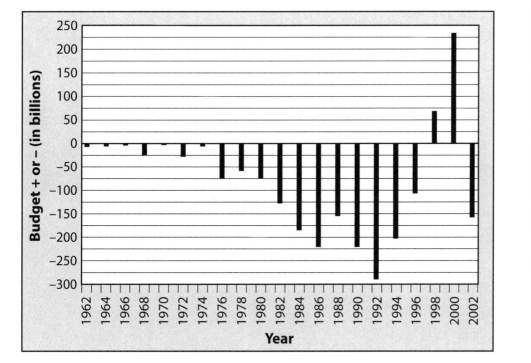

6. In what year was the U.S. budget deficit the greatest?

A. 1962
B. 1972
C. 1982
D. 1992

7. In what year was the budget deficit closest to zero?

A. 1960
B. 1970
C. 1980
D. 1990

8. Between what years was there the greatest change?

A. between 1994 and 1996
B. between 1996 and 1998
C. between 1998 and 2000
D. between 2000 and 2002

9. In what year did the U.S. economy have the most money?

A. 2002
B. 2000
C. 1998
D. 1996

10. In which years did the U.S. **not** have a deficit?

A. 1968 and 1970
B. 1978 and 1980
C. 1988 and 1990
D. 1998 and 2000

HOW DID YOU DO? Count the number of correct answers on your answer sheet. Record this number in the bar graph on the inside back cover.

Spotlight: Reading

A Read the questions in the chart below and predict the answers. Then read the information below the chart and look for the answers to the questions.

Questions	My answers before reading the text	My answers after reading the text
1) What is the European Union?		
2) When did Europe go to a single currency?		
3) Which economy has the highest unemployment, the E.U. or the U.S.?		
4) Which economy has the highest inflation rate, the E.U. or the U.S.?		

A Tale of Two Economies

In 1992 the Treaty of Maastricht instituted new forms of cooperation between members of the European Economic Community, thereby establishing a single economic system known as the European Union. It was also the year that Europe adopted a single currency, the Euro. Originally the E.U. was a partnership of 15 member nations, but 10 new countries joined in 2004. In eliminating trade and employment barriers, the E.U. created a single market that threatened to dominate the American economy.

Has that happened? Not yet, according to 2003 figures. The E.U. of 25 countries has a much larger population, although it is smaller in size. The United States imports a greater percentage of the world's imports (22.9%) than does the E.U. (14%), while the two economies are similar in their shares of world exports (13.8% and 13.1%). Stronger economies generally export more than they import. This would suggest that the E.U. has the advantage.

Other economic indicators tell a different story, however. In general, a relatively low rate of inflation and unemployment signals a healthy economy. The inflation rate in the E.U. was 2%, but only 1.6% in the United States. The rate of unemployment in the United States was 6.0%, whereas in the E.U. it was 9.1%. These figures suggest that the U.S. is still stronger economically according to these measures.

Although the single market of the European Union has given member nations definite advantages economically over the old multiple economies, time will tell if this new market is strong enough to overtake the economy of the United States.

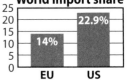

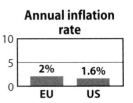

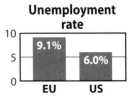

B Underline the words or phrases in the article on page 158 that show comparison, and circle those that show contrast. Write the words or phrases in the chart.

Comparison	Contrast

C List your ideas about the two economies in the Venn Diagram.

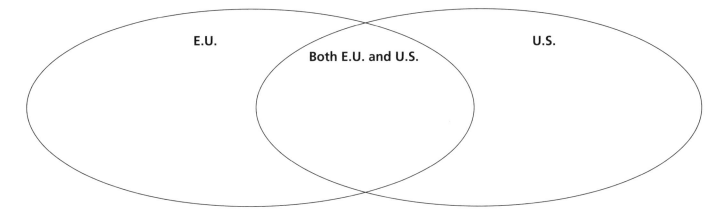

E.U.

Both E.U. and U.S.

U.S.

D Answer the questions.

1. In what way(s) is the U.S. economy stronger than the economy of the E.U.?

_____

_____

_____

2. In what way(s) is the E.U. economy stronger?

_____

_____

_____

3. How can the creation of the European Union help the countries that belong to it economically?

_____

_____

_____

Spotlight: Writing

A Write the transition words and phrases in the appropriate places in the chart.

also	and	as a result	because
besides	but	consequently	conversely
despite	due to	even though	first
for example	for instance	for this reason	further
furthermore	however	in addition	instead of
in spite of	like	moreover	nevertheless
on the other hand	second	so	such as
therefore	third	though	thus
too	whereas	yet	

To add information	To show order	To show cause and effect

To give an example	To show a contrast	

B Complete the paragraph with appropriate transition words.

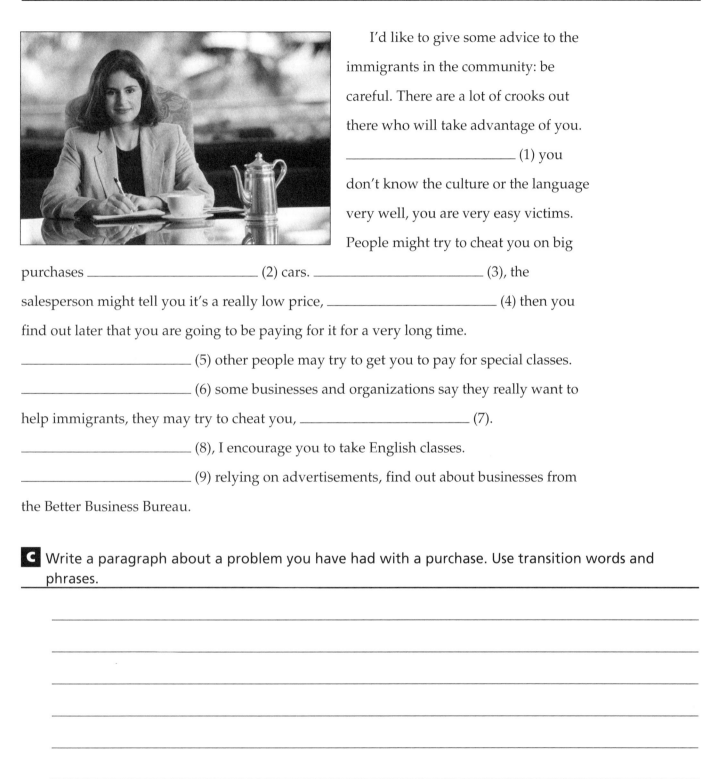

I'd like to give some advice to the immigrants in the community: be careful. There are a lot of crooks out there who will take advantage of you. _____ (1) you don't know the culture or the language very well, you are very easy victims. People might try to cheat you on big purchases _____ (2) cars. _____ (3), the salesperson might tell you it's a really low price, _____ (4) then you find out later that you are going to be paying for it for a very long time. _____ (5) other people may try to get you to pay for special classes. _____ (6) some businesses and organizations say they really want to help immigrants, they may try to cheat you, _____ (7). _____ (8), I encourage you to take English classes. _____ (9) relying on advertisements, find out about businesses from the Better Business Bureau.

C Write a paragraph about a problem you have had with a purchase. Use transition words and phrases.

_____

_____

_____

_____

_____

_____

_____

_____

Correlation Table

Student Book Pages	Workbook Pages	Student Book Pages	Workbook Pages
Unit 1		**Unit 3**	
4–5	2–3	40–41	42–43
6–7	4–5	42–43	44–45
8–9	6–7	44–45	46–47
10–11	8–9	46–47	48–49
12–13	10–11	48–49	50–51
14–15	12–15	50–51	52–55
16–17	16–17	52–53	56–57
18–19	18–19	54–55	58–59
20–21	20–21	56–57	60–61
Unit 2		**Unit 4**	
22–23	22–23	58–59	62–63
24–25	24–25	60–61	64–65
26–27	26–27	62–63	66–67
28–29	28–29	64–65	68–69
30–31	30–33	66–67	70–71
32–33	34–35	68–69	72–75
34–35	36–37	70–71	76–77
36–37	38–39	72–73	78–79
38–39	40–41	74–75	80–81

Student Book Pages	Workbook Pages
Unit 5	
76–77	82–83
78–79	84–85
80–81	86–87
82–83	88–89
84–85	90–91
86–87	92–95
88–89	96–97
90–91	98–99
92–93	100–101
Unit 6	
94–95	102–103
96–97	104–105
98–99	106–107
100–101	108–109
102–103	110–111
104–105	112–115
106–107	116–117
108–109	118–119
110–111	120–121

Student Book Pages	Workbook Pages
Unit 7	
112–113	122–123
114–115	124–125
116–117	126–127
118–119	128–129
120–121	130–131
122–123	132–135
124–125	136–137
126–127	138–139
128–129	140–141
Unit 8	
130–131	142–143
132–133	144–145
134–135	146–147
136–137	148–149
138–139	150–151
140–141	152–155
142–143	156–157
144–145	158–159
146–147	160–161

Photo Credits

UNIT 3, PAGE 52
Work Application Lesson
Activity A, Answer Key

Workers' Health and Safety Quiz

Activity A, Page 52.

1. Workers in the United States do NOT have the right to remove uncomfortable safety equipment.

2. Sprains and strains, usually involving the back, are the most common workplace injury.

3. False. Your boss cannot fire you for refusing to do unsafe work.

4. The construction industry has the most workplace fatalities.

5. False. Office workers DO have to worry about getting injured at work. Jobs that require repetitive motion such as typing or scanning groceries can cause serious injury to the hands and arms.